Lecture Notes in Artificial Intelligence   3890

Edited by J. G. Carbonell and J. Siekmann

Subseries of Lecture Notes in Computer Science

T0218660

Simon G. Thompson
Robert Ghanea-Hercock (Eds.)

Defence Applications of Multi-Agent Systems

International Workshop, DAMAS 2005
Utrecht, The Netherlands, July 25, 2005
Revised and Invited Papers

 Springer

Series Editors

Jaime G. Carbonell, Carnegie Mellon University, Pittsburgh, PA, USA
Jörg Siekmann, University of Saarland, Saarbrücken, Germany

Volume Editors

Simon G. Thompson
Robert Ghanea-Hercock
BT Labs, Adastral Park, MLB1 PP12
Martlesham, Ipswich IP5 3RE, UK
E-mail: {simon.2.thompson, robert.ghanea-hercock}@bt.com

Library of Congress Control Number: 2006921551

CR Subject Classification (1998): I.2.11, I.2, C.2.4, D.2, I.6.8, F.3

LNCS Sublibrary: SL 7 – Artificial Intelligence

ISSN   0302-9743
ISBN-10   3-540-32832-7 Springer Berlin Heidelberg New York
ISBN-13   978-3-540-32832-2 Springer Berlin Heidelberg New York

Springer is a part of Springer Science+Business Media

springer.com

© Springer-Verlag Berlin Heidelberg 2006
Printed in Germany

Typesetting: Camera-ready by author, data conversion by Scientific Publishing Services, Chennai, India
Printed on acid-free paper   SPIN: 11683704   06/3142   5 4 3 2 1 0

Preface

The evolution of defense processes towards network-enabled systems and rapid deployment scenarios, as exemplified by the UK Network Enabled Capability (NEC) program or the US Network Centric Warfare (NCW) effort, is creating an urgent demand for highly adaptive and autonomous information support systems. These are large-scale organizational and technological transformational processes. There is therefore a requirement to create autonomous IT infrastructures with automated logistics and planning capability, all of which provides significant scope for an agent-based approach.

The emerging problem set in the defense ICT domain is also mirrored in the civil sector for enterprise scale systems, where cost reduction, legacy integration, scalability and security, are all significant problems to be addressed. To date, the civil sector has taken the lead on the application of agent systems, particularly in the manufacturing sector, (e.g., [Jennings & Bussmann 2003]). Recently, agent systems have become significant mainstream ICT technologies with the emergence of IBM's autonomic computing initiative and the integration of agent technology in various products for infrastructure management. Further information on civilian applications of agent technology can be found in the AAMAS industrial applications conference proceedings [Pechoucek et al. 2005].

Of course, the defense domain has the additional problems resulting from hostile actors and environments. However, it is precisely this aspect that makes a multi-agent system (MAS) approach attractive as it offers increased resilience, run-time flexibility, and embedded intelligence. In addition the key factors in the evolution of MAS have been the advent of service-oriented computing, high-power computing capability, and high-speed ubiquitous networks, which have finally created a suitably rich electronic environment for MAS to be deployed to full effect.

The defense domain therefore covers a broad spectrum of applications that will benefit from an agent approach, including:

ISTAR – sensing and information fusion management
C3 – agent-based command and control support and analysis
NEC/NCW – agent-based middleware and P2P networks
UAVs and Autonomous Robots
Self-Organizing Systems and networks
Simulation and Scenario Engines
Real-time Logistics and Planning support

As we enter the next phase of networked warfare up to 2020, the need for self-organizing, self-healing and intelligent ICT support systems and networks will become paramount. The roadmap to achieve this vision of NEC/NCW is heavily reliant on the fullest utilization of multi-agent systems.

This book is a post-proceedings for the Defence Applications of Multi-Agent Systems (DAMAS) workshop held at the Autonomous Agents and Multi-Agents System conference (AAMAS) in Utrecht in June 2005 (http://www.aamas2005.nl). It contains versions of selected papers presented at the workshop which have been updated and extended by the authors in the light of the comments and discussion of their work.

The workshop was cross-disciplinary in nature, bringing together researchers from academic, industrial, and defense teams. The goals of the workshop were to explore the value of agent technology in defense applications and to review example agent systems applied to defense applications. The book therefore represents a cross-section of the current state of the art in defense applications of agent systems.

The workshop featured several lively discussions on the presentations and the challenges that the defense domain held for agent technology. These are summarized in the first invited paper in this collection, by Beautement et al.

Part 1 contains several papers on decision support and simulation. This includes a contribution on maritime situation awareness by Hemaissa et al., which present an innovative approach based on multi-agent negotiation to fuse classifiers, using the flexibility and reliability of a multi-agent system to exploit distributed data across dispersed sources. The following paper by Louvieris et al outlines the application of Bayesian technologies to CSF (critical success factors) assessment for parsimonious military decision making using an agent-based decision support system. This paper illustrates the application of CSF-enabled Bayesian belief networks (BBN) technology through an agent-based paradigm for assessing the likelihood of success of military missions. A paper by Wise et al. considers whether an agent-based autonomic network control system can provide the flexibility needed to allow an agile mission group to reconfigure their network, while maintaining a high tempo, yet minimize their demands on signals staff. Their architecture describes services that configure a device, and a hierarchy of networks, in terms of the contribution that each makes to networks of which it is a member.

The next paper in this section by Parunak et al. considers the importance of modelling emotion within a simulated combat environment in order to provide a realistic simulation of the likely behavior of forces in battle. The models developed simulate the propagation of emotion in combat units using concepts from Agent technology such as pheromones in a computationally tractable and realistic training simulator.

Part 2 looks at UAVs and starts with a paper from Han et al. which discusses how three technologies can be combined to achieve the UAV functionality needed for coordinated autonomous operation, from building up accurate beliefs, efficiently gathering information, to acting rationally. It discusses how, in order to facilitate the target-tracking activity, a reliable information provisioning network can be constructed by selecting the most appropriate information sources and using trust evaluations to perform belief revision. Also, a macro-based action selection scheme is deployed for efficient coordination of target-tracking activity among agents.

This is followed by a paper from Dasgupta et al. on the interesting problem of automatic target recognition using a multi-agent swarm of unmanned aerial vehicles.

The aim being to avoid a centralized approach to UAV direction. The UAVs employ a swarming algorithm implemented through software agents to congregate at and identify targets.

Part 3 considers wider system management issues such as security and the logistics domain. The paper by Janicke et al. presents a security model that allows the expression of dynamic access control policies that can change on time and events. A simple agent system, simulating a platoon, is used to show the need and the advantages of our policy model. The paper finally describes how existing tool-support can be used for the analysis and verification.

A paper by Greene et al. covers the critical topic of intelligent logistics support using an agent approach. They present a novel cognitive agent architecture and demonstrate its effectiveness in the sense and respond logistics (SRL) domain. Effective applications to support SRL must anticipate and adapt to emerging situations and other dynamic military operations. SRL transforms the static, hierarchical architectures of traditional military models into re-configurable networks designed to encourage coordination among small peer units. This is followed by work from Carvalho et al., who present a mobile agent-based middleware that supports both point-to-point message and hierarchical data-stream communications in these environments. Two infrastructure technologies (Mockets and FlexFeed) are introduced as service providers for messaging and publish-subscriber models for data streaming. Opportunistic resource allocation and monitoring are handled by distributed coordination algorithms, implemented here through two complementary technologies (Stand-In Agents and Acquaintance models).

The final paper by Allsop is an invited contribution that considers the technical challenges that remain in realizing the potential of agent-based technologies in the defense arena.

Organizing the DAMAS workshop and producing this volume of proceedings was a difficult, time-consuming, but ultimately very rewarding exercise (or so we hope). It would have been far harder without the support, advice, and assistance of others. Most significantly no event of this type can occur without the support of the community in the form of contributed papers and presentations, and in the form of reviewing. All the presented papers at DAMAS were reviewed by at least two anonymous reviewers in the Program Committee, and we would like to take this opportunity to thank them for the quality of the reviews they produced and for the timely fashion in which they produced them. It is worth stressing that the nature of the DAMAS Program Committee makes this an even more noteworthy point than would normally be the case in a workshop. The DAMAS PC was made up of members that are all actively involved in defense projects and many of the members are senior people in major commercial organizations, and the demands made on their time make taking on a duty like reviewing for a workshop especially onerous.

In addition we would like to thank Nick Jennings and Mark Greaves for their assistance in organizing the workshop and acting as senior Program Committee members. Both of them were instrumental in making the event happen, and their advice and council did much to shape the workshops character and content. Andre Meyer provided us with much-needed support in making the necessary local arrangements for the workshop and we would also like to thank him for his diligence and for the support he provided.

Finally we would like to thank the organizers of AAMAS 2005 for agreeing to host DAMAS, in particular Frank Dignum and Rino Falcone.

January 2006   Robert Ghanea-Hercock
Simon Thompson

N. R. Jennings and S. Bussmann (2003) "Agent-based control systems" *IEEE Control Systems Magazine* 23 (3) 61-74.
Pechoucek, M., Steiner, D. Thompson, S.G. (eds) *Industrial Applications of Autonomous Agents.* ACM July 2005.

Program Committee

Table of Contents

Part III: Systems and Security

Invited Paper

Autonomous Agents and Multi-agent Systems (AAMAS) for the Military — Issues and Challenges

Patrick Beautement[1], David Allsopp[1], Mark Greaves[2], Steve Goldsmith[3], Shannon Spires[3], Simon G. Thompson[4], and Helge Janicke[5]

[1] QinetiQ Ltd
pbeautement@qinetiq.com, dnallsopp@qinetiq.com
[2] Vulcan
markg@vulcan.com
[3] Sandia National Labs
sygolds@sandia.gov, svspire@sandia.gov
[4] BT
simon.2.thompson@bt.com
[5] DMU
heljanic@dmu.ac.uk

Abstract. The military domain is a very challenging environment and human endeavour in this domain is characterized by uncertainty and the need to be able to deal with significant and disruptive dynamic changes. In addition, activities are driven by human decision-makers who need support in making sense of the environment and with reasoning about, and effecting, possible futures. Hence, various unique factors need to be taken into account when considering the provision of applications, tools, devices and infrastructure for the military domain. This paper will itemize and discuss some of these factors in the context of autonomous agents and multi-agent systems. This paper is a desiderata for the research space.

1 The Military Context

The military domain is a very challenging environment characterized by uncertainty and the need to be able to deal with significant and disruptive dynamic changes. Despite an increasing trend towards adopting approaches from the commercial domain, military activities are different in one key respect - there are opponents who are doing their best to frustrate or destroy friendly activities and to deflect or subvert allies or neutral actors. This means that nothing can be relied upon and that therefore key capabilities include: the ability to dynamically adapt to (or shape) change; to be agile (and grasp fleeting opportunities) and be robust (in the face of potentially catastrophic disruption). Anything that inhibits these capabilities is unacceptable.

In addition, military activities are driven by human decision-makers who need support in making sense of the environment and with reasoning about, and effecting, possible futures. Conflict is, essentially, a human activity. Admittedly, all creatures on the planet are involved in a competition for resources including all those involved in commerce. Conflict, however, is different in that it always involves the purposeful disruption / destruction of the affairs of your opponents - driven by the intent of a

S.G. Thompson and R. Ghanea-Hercock (Eds.): DAMAS 2005, LNAI 3890, pp. 1–13, 2006.
© Springer-Verlag Berlin Heidelberg 2006

state, group or individual. Consequently, when supporting these human-led endeavours, the primacy of the human must always be kept at the forefront. Three other key aspects of the military domain are:

1. the certainty of uncertainty;
2. the inherent heterogeneity and complexity of the environment; and
3. the increasing blurring of boundaries between self and non-self (including friends, foes and other actors).

When reasoning about conflict one should always start by embracing the realization that nothing will be absolutely predictable and that being able to cope with uncertainty should be a fundamental capability. An aspect of this is the heterogeneity and complexity of the environment. Conflict with an opponent on a 'standardized' battle space will end up being an attrition war in some limited part of the conflict space. Instead, finding asymmetries (where you are strong and so can wield decisive advantage against an opponent) is an important strategy. This involves working with anything in the battle space which can be wielded as a weapon, including exploiting (even deliberately increasing) the complexity of the environment to undermine the opponent. The key is to always retain as big a range of options as possible (from which to generate novelty) as this is the counter to uncertainty. Finally, cyberspace is a battlespace in its own right (not just a conduit for communication between people). It is a domain closed to humans and so 'cyberspace dominance' can only be obtained by using proxies to wield power on our behalf – those proxies are software agents.

2 Previous Work

Autonomous Agents and Multi-Agent System (AAMAS) are computer software systems that exhibit one or both of the following two tightly coupled behaviours. An Agent is exhibiting Autonomous behaviour when it makes a decision as to what goals it will attempt to fulfil, or when it is able to choose between a number of different strategies to fulfil those goals. Multi-Agent behaviour is exhibited when Agents co-ordinate their behaviour in order to achieve their common or separately held but coupled goals. An extensive literature is available which describes work that has been undertaken with the object of understanding and developing such systems (for example Rosenschein et-al 2003; Jennings et-al 2004; Dignum et-al 2005, Pechoucek et-al 2005).

Domains which are particularly amenable to solutions that use AAMAS technology have been categorized (Jennings & Wooldridge 1998) as being :

- open systems : systems with structures that evolve over time, are unknown in advance and are heterogeneous (the result of the actions of different actors independently and dependently)
- complex systems : characterized by Jennings and Wooldridge as systems that are too complex to understand without modularization
- ubiquitous computing systems : which require interaction with all other actors in their environment in various contexts. Systems of this sort require interaction interfaces that go beyond the enumeration of the required behaviour and instead co-operate with users to achieve goals.

All of the elements of this categorization intersect with the military context described above, so it is no surprise that there have been a number of attempts to utilize AAMAS technology in the Military Context, for example:

- CoABS / CoAX (Allsopp et-al 2002) : A project to develop AAMAS technology into an integrated environment to provide adjustable interoperability between disparate information systems and to support distributed mixed-initiative decision-making with acceptable agent behaviour (Bradshaw 2004). It used the CoABS Grid which is a well developed infrastructure that has been evaluated and tested in several operational military settings.
- DAML: The DARPA Agent Markup Language. DAML is a project to develop data, information and knowledge formats for exchange between systems. The DAML+OIL language has been extended and refined into the OWL ontology language adopted by the W3C and used in projects like the AKT (Shadbolt et-al 2004).
- UltraLog (Bates 2005) utilizes agent technology to provide highly survivable information and logistics systems. UltraLog was independently verified as being able to offer a high degree of robustness while solving problems of a realistic size and nature. The Cougaar agent tool kit (Helsinger & Wright 2005) was a result of the UltraLog program and is now opensource and widely used.
- FCS Command and Control Study (Potok et-al 2003) analyzes the current state of agent-based technology applied to C2 functions for the Future Combat System and net-centric warfare in general. The study concludes that advances are required in the areas of scalability, mobility and security of agent systems before the command and control problem can be suitably addressed.

But it is our contention that the uptake and impact of AAMAS technology in the military domain remains disappointing. In particular it is a puzzle as to why AAMAS technology, which is aimed at providing abstractions and tools for handling open, pervasive and complex situations has not become the technology of choice to implement new doctrines which advocate ad-hoc, agile and decentralized organization. Also, the missions that the military now face (including small scale short notice deployments, complex coalition force structures, counter terrorism and disaster relief) all seem to require from information systems the kind of behaviours that AAMAS technologies offer.

The rest of this paper in part attempts to explain this situation, and in part attempts to provide a list of pitfalls and pratfalls that the developers of military applications (who want to exploit AAMAS technologies) should consider.

3 General Issues Around Agent and AAMAS Implementation

This paper is aimed specifically at the military context, but lessons from AAMAS development in commercial and scientific applications must not be ignored by teams focusing on military requirements. Pitfalls identified in this area (Wooldridge and Jennings 1998) can be summarized as:

Political:
  overselling,
  dogmatic commitment to AAMAS technology.
User context:
  failure to understand the military domain,
  failure to address scale and tempo of real operations,
  failure to match the technology to the constraints of a real military environment.
Management:
  lack of technical appreciation of AAMAS technology,
  lack of application understanding,
  failure to differentiate between prototypes and systems.
Conceptual:
  using buzzwords without understanding them,
  AAMAS as a silver bullet.
Analytical:
  over genericism,
  a failure of analogy.
Agent level:
  failure to reuse architectural principles,
  inappropriate emphasis on problem solving as opposed to usability,
  over-simplification (assumptions about clear boundaries and identification of self and non-self),
  failure to use proper granularity to model the system.
Implementation:
  legacy system integration,
  failure to abide by de-facto standards.

These strap lines highlight "anti-patterns" of AAMAS development that have become well known to commercial developers. In addition we would add that in recent years it has become clear that a lack of trained development staff, a lack of systematic methodological tools and a lack of case studies that could be used to enable and support business cases, have also hampered military and commercial development. The rest of this paper focuses on the issues that are particularly significant when attempting to transfer AAMAS technology to the military sphere.

4 Key Issues

Given the context described above it is clear that there will be some key challenges and issues for anyone wishing to employ agents (of any type) in the military domain. These arise from the need to embrace uncertainty, lack of boundaries, complexity and heterogeneity and to recognize the primacy of the human in military endeavours. In this part of the paper we itemize and comment on some of these key issues, indicating some of the factors which apply to them.

4.1   Analysis, Requirements and Politics

These are the issues that must be considered when starting or contemplating a particular AAMAS project for the military. If these issues are not considered at an early stage it is likely that the artefacts produced by the project, while possibly attractive in terms of research or perceived value add, will not be suited for real world military use.

Understand the Role of Command in Setting the Shape of the Organization

It is important to understand the creative dynamic which exists between top-down intent and bottom-up mission command. Command creates the conditions for organizations to form, adapt and flourish - to be purposeful. In addition, it is important to recognize the role of self-regulation and bottom-up emergence in maintaining organizational viability and agility. The required collective behaviours cannot all be programmed top-down (Stalinist control). In reality, organizational structures are dynamic and are often built on patterns derived from trained 'templates'. Hence, in reality, operational units and agents will be loosely coupled - this is especially true in a coalition where there are many different restraints, constraints and sensitivities which prevent tight binding. This loose coupling is a source of many important properties such as the ability to generate novel behaviours and to be resilient. System architectures must therefore take the organizational change within the military into account and go away from centralized approaches toward loosely coupled, responsive (to events) and self monitoring components.

Understand the Need to be Able to Grasp the Fleeting Opportunity

The leaders involved in the execution of operations work under mission command and must be able to grab fleeting opportunities as they present themselves. The computer must not force them to adhere to 'the plan' at all costs (especially as this is a mixed-initiative issue). An example here might be, opportunistically, finding yourself driving by the enemy's computer centre in your tanks and not hitting it because it's not in the plan! Any successful application must allow the human user to intervene at any point in time and then immediately adapt to the changes that may arise from the interaction. The control must remain with the human at any point in time.

See the Decision-makers as Active Drivers of Change

It is important to facilitate people to be active decision-makers not dumb process-followers and to recognize that the majority of command activities are informal and event-driven and cannot be captured as mechanistic process models. Instead of delivering "the right information at the right place at the right time" (you can never work out in advance what / who / when / where 'right' will be), enable decision-makers to get what they want, when they need it, in the form they want. This involves really understanding the dynamics of decision-making - that there are thousands of nested, interdependent, loosely-coupled Observe, Orientate, Decide, Act (OODA) loops running at any one time (even OODA loops are nested OODA loops - though this is rarely shown). Decision-makers must be able to exploit the advantages of loose coupling to reconfigure in response to threats and opportunities.

Realize that Conflict is never the Same Twice

Hence, it is usually difficult to define repeatable processes (if you do, it leads to inflexibility). This strongly contrasts to commercial settings where businesses strive for repeatable processes to optimise their operations and conform to regulatory requirements. It is important to characterize the invariants of conflict and consider the real space of potential challenges that might have to be faced. For example, this means realizing that conflict is increasingly 'strange', where the enemy forces (if you can identify them) are increasingly employing our own assets against ourselves on an ill-defined 'battlefield' (so-called 'war among the people'). Out of this change the need arises for the system to constantly evolve. However, system evolution is difficult and needs to be controlled, since it may lead to unwanted system behaviour. Any technology employed in this problem space must address this issue, to be competitive in future conflicts.

Focus on Execution, not Planning

Planning is a way of trying to reduce the uncertainty of the future, but is not a substitute for having the ability to execute dynamically and with agility at run-time (because no plan survives contact with the enemy). Over-emphasis on planning processes and planning tools (as seen in Gulf War II) is a current weakness. Plans are really just shared artefacts that aid reasoning and communication between people, but they tend to become an end in themselves - they are poor substitutes for the dynamic thinking which formed them. Also, there are various levels of planning with different time horizons and concerns (i.e. there is not a single monolithic plan). So, being able to reactively re-plan is one approach in which execution support tools and infrastructures enable dynamic opportunistic adaptation during execution.

Work with Systems which Cannot be Bounded Tightly

Most real-world activities do not have tightly defined boundaries. Instead perceived boundaries are porous because in reality there is not a clear division between us and them. 'We' are merely a loose assemblage of actors sharing a common purpose. Indeed, agents need to be able to operate in loose teams / groups changing between roles and varying relationships as flexibly as humans do. The ad-hoc nature of these coalitions makes it necessary to cope with the arising security implications. Passing information/technology to a friend that may be tomorrow's foe is a major concern in coalitions that exists only for a short period of time. Systems must be able to cope with these implications, or at least empower human decision makers to incorporate this information in their decision making process.

Accept that Losing is a form of Learning

Discomfort is good and drives change. Losing generates discomfort. Opportunities generate discomfort and drive change too. During training, it is better not to work in the 'fitness' part of the space, but start with unfitness / discomfort and consider how to reduce / mitigate it. Making that journey generates learning. We may need to deliberately force that journey on Multi-agent Systems (MAS) to develop their capabilities (through co-evolution driven by predator / prey competition etc).

4.2 Implementation

These are the issues that must be considered by any team that has been provided with a list of functional requirements for an application in the military domain. Also considered below are the non functional tripwires that turn a good idea with funding into a waste of money and time.

Test your System using Military Metrics

Military metrics are often ignored, but should include things such as: speed of command, operational availability and agility (tempo). The whole process of testing needs to be re-thought out. There is often no proper test plan (there may be a cool demo but no evidence of applicability to a range of potential challenges). Verification and Validation activities should not only be constrained to take place during the development phase, but should constantly verify that the system during run-time executes within acceptable boundaries. This requirement originates from the complexity of the environment which cannot be simulated under laboratory conditions.

Enable your Agents to work in the operational Military Computing Environment

Just as commercial implementations of AAMAS technology are rarely greenfield applications with an unlimited processing, memory and bandwidth budget, the military environment is technically very challenging. Applications which do not acknowledge this and are not able to work within these constraints are useless, which implies:

- *Be able to work with Constrained Resources.* Tactical communications are the reality (as is variation in quality of service). This means that the ability to sense and adapt dynamically to resource availability is important. It should also be possible to see if resources are being expended on housekeeping or on the main mission etc.
- *Be able to work with Partial Information.* Waiting for a 100% solution is bad. Also, you probably won't know what you would like to know in advance - especially at design-time. So agents should be able to work with poor quality data and understand the nature of the military problem better. This will include being able to work with un-trusted information - which may not only be partial, but can be wrong or misleading, especially when security of parts of the system is compromised. A successful system offers support in recognizing such inconsistencies.
- *Don't assume a Commercial Context.* The military environment is not only resource-limited but also brutal. So, anticipate unreliable comm.-unications, indifferent line-of-sight, variable availability of band-width / quality of service and poor power supplies etc. This applies not only to the internal operation of the system, but also affects the human-computer interface design. Systems must maintain an acceptable level of usability under extreme circumstances.
- *Understand the Technical / Software context.* The tempo and intensity of military operations means that you may be talking to vast COTS databases (not just MySQL) and integration issues might not just be technical, but architectural. A typical problem solving mode in legacy systems is to move information out of computer systems into human-led workflows. However, too much emphasis on COTS and legacy wrapping may not get you ahead of the opponent. One of the inherent problems with COTS products is that you must modify your business processes (or, more to the point, your *warfighting* processes) to meet the limitations of the products.

The degree to which this is necessary must be critically analyzed as to how it impacts your warfighting posture. When these limitations are factored in, COTS may *cost* more than custom solutions.

- *Can you Scale to deal with real-world problems?* Military applications often require 1000s+ of agents. So, as an example, to understand the scale required consider the a typical force structure deployed in a recent military operation of UK troops in Sierra-Leone: 1 regiment of marines, 1 battalion airborne, 6 battalions infantry and 7 regiments of support troops (engineers etc); in total up to 4000 UK troops were deployed (Hansard 2000) and these required support to remain active in the field.

- *Availability and Reliability.* Computation has to be on-line 24/7 and can not be stopped for maintenance (can't go off-line, debug, update and restart during an operation). Instead, we need to obtain robustness through exploiting redundancy and replace-ability. Note therefore that safety, security and reliability are not optional add-ons but must be anticipated from the early design of the system. When replacing components, it must be ensured that the overall system cannot be knocked out by a rogue / faulty component. See "single point of failure" below.

- *Avoid Single Points of Failure and expect things to Fail.* Assume that single points will inevitably fail. Avoid a fortress mentality. Don't assume perfect infrastructure and full availability.

- *Enable Robustness and Resilience from the Start.* Robustness and resilience should be displayed in the face of malicious / rogue agents (including failure / compromise) etc. Hence, all designs should consider cyber security (Gorodetsky & Kotenko 2002, Kotenko 2003) and especially intrusion tolerance (Wang et-al 2001, Atighetchi et-al 2004) as primary requirements.

- *Assume the existence of bugs - but still design a way that things can succeed (enable graceful degradation, regeneration and recovery).* This should include things such as the ability to recognise and survive infrastructure attack and should include providing abilities to detect and repair at run-time in an autonomic way.

Technology Acquisition (Procurement) Issues

The MAS community should be realistic about the degree of change that can occur in the military domain in the shorter-term (however, note that if we are too similar to the opponent, or cannot display novelty at run-time, then we will not have a decisive advantage). Also:

- *Be aware of, but not intimidated by, the acquisition bureaucracy.* Look at how novel hardware is introduced, learn the strategies and apply them to MAS (understand why software acquisition is so different). NB: For example, Network-centric Warfare (NCW) has been embraced - how was that achieved and is there anything that we can learn from its spread? Most importantly, NCW (and the recent book "Power to the Edge" [Alberts & Haynes 2003]) have set the context and clear requirement for ad-hoc networks and agility etc of the sort well suited to MAS.

- *Target parts of the military (such as the marines) that may be more suitable / open to prototypes and the introduction of novelty.* Customers are unlikely to gamble their organizations on an untried technology no matter how compelling the cases that are made in theory (although as noted above NCW seems to be the exception to prove the rule)
- *Work from case studies that prove the requirement.* Gulf War II showed how much adaptive resource management (in all domains, including cyberspace) is required (Talbot 2004). Deployments to Bosnia (where sensor grids were deployed), Kosovo (where there were coordination difficulties), Somalia (where the wrong information was being gathered) and recent relief operations have shown how support for agile and interoperable infrastructures is in demand. Applications focused on requirements like these have a starting point from which procurement cases can be constructed.

4.3 Operation

Operational issues are factors that AAMAS systems will encounter when they are running in a military application; they are the issues that derail systems that would do the same job effectively if they were implemented in a civilian environment (a company or a government office for instance) but fail in the military context. These are a problem for commercial agent systems in the way that jamming and encryption are a problem for GSM communications on the battlefield.

Avoid Optimization, Efficiency and Predictability

Optimum solutions are not necessarily the best, neither is being predictable. If you can compute and predict something, so can your opponent - they will then use the information to be there to defeat you. What is important is keeping the maximum amount of option space open - as it is from this option space that commanders generate the novelty they need to deal with the uncertainty of operations. Hence, we should accept that uncertainty is the norm and all our designs should start from this point.

Minimize Design-time Assumptions to Maximize Run-time Adaptability

We should provide at design-time organizational units (agent teams) with properties which, when activated at run-time, enable the required novelty and adaptability to be displayed. We should also construct run-time tools which have the ability to shape things in cyberspace dynamically. We should strive to provide capabilities which enable us to dynamically integrate complementary, yet diverse, elements (especially legacy) on demand.

Expect the Opponent to be Robust and Competent

Include the opponent in all your considerations. That way, failure will be expected (see vulnerabilities below):

- *Consider the Vulnerabilities that you are Exposing to an Opponent through the use of your Technology.* Spend time considering the vulnerabilities of your approach - how could what you are doing be exploited and subverted by a malicious opponent, disaffected personnel or self-inflicted SNAFUs (remember you may actually be the one introducing the vulnerability - we'd be safer without your big idea). Expect your strategies and approaches to be turned to malicious purpose. Consider the outrageous likely. Consider countermeasures / self-healing.

- *Be Aware of the Multiplicity of Routes for Attack.* Network-centric approaches are connecting previously disparate elements. This means that the consequences of attacks can cascade through from the physical, to the information / software and up to the social / cultural domains - so that attacks result in consequences which are manifested far away from the point where they were originally 'felt'.

4.4   Some Ideas About Key Application Areas

Given the context described above it is possible to identify some key areas for the application of AAMAS. The AAMAS context sees cyberspace as a conduit for communication between people, it is a domain inhabited by active entities which can augment human capabilities by becoming part of the team. Hence, tasks can be delegated to these entities and, as a result, human cognitive load can be reduced. In addition, many housekeeping and resource adaptation tasks can be handed off to cyberspace which can then do a great deal of self-regulation. The range of technologies involved and their relationship to human users are shown in Fig. 1.

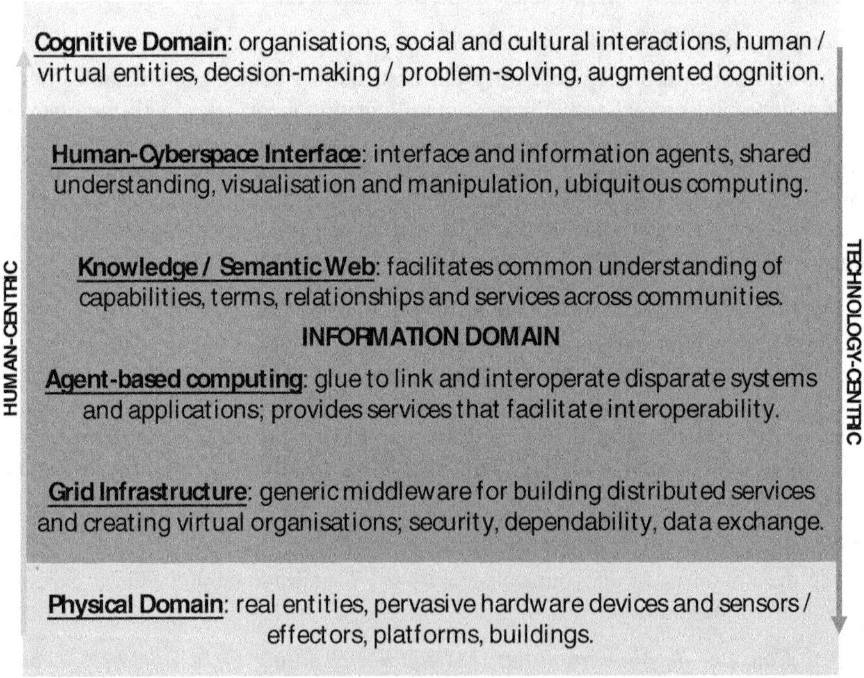

Cognitive Domain: organisations, social and cultural interactions, human / virtual entities, decision-making / problem-solving, augmented cognition.

Human-Cyberspace Interface: interface and information agents, shared understanding, visualisation and manipulation, ubiquitous computing.

Knowledge / Semantic Web: facilitates common understanding of capabilities, terms, relationships and services across communities.

INFORMATION DOMAIN

Agent-based computing: glue to link and interoperate disparate systems and applications; provides services that facilitate interoperability.

Grid Infrastructure: generic middleware for building distributed services and creating virtual organisations; security, dependability, data exchange.

Physical Domain: real entities, pervasive hardware devices and sensors / effectors, platforms, buildings.

HUMAN-CENTRIC

TECHNOLOGY-CENTRIC

Fig. 1. The interaction of a technology centric and a human centric view of the military domain

The list below is not exhaustive but is intended to indicate that significant value can be added by MAS in the following areas:

- *Providing Agent-mediated Interfaces.* Human beings distribute cognition load into their environment [Hollan 2000] as a way of increasing effectiveness and to facilitate teamworking. Currently, many of our IT systems inhibit this behaviour and, as a result, actually reduce human capabilities. MAS support the kind of load-sharing which can augment human capabilities as they can act as taskable team members (albeit limited ones) [Bradshaw 2004].

- *For Self-regulation and / or Enabling Autonomic Behaviour.* MAS, as a digital society, can self-regulate behaviour on behalf of human beings, for example by adapting to the sudden failure of a computing resource (for example [Hoile et-al 2002]) This kind of self-healing and self-adaptation has been neatly captured in IBM's so-called 'autonomic computing' initiatives. These cover things such as throttling destructive cascades of effects - where there isn't time to wait for the humans to notice what's happening. These are key capabilities because as human beings we need proxies which can act purposefully in cyberspace on our behalf - only MAS can do this.

- *Providing Adaptive 'Middleware' Wrappers capable of Mixed Initiative Interaction.* MAS can be used to wrap monolithic / legacy software in such a way as to appear as if they are agent-based and hence exposing the possibility of novel (useful) functionality (eg putting a multi-agent responsive UI around legacy monoliths). This wrapping enables the legacy systems to engage in limited dialogue with agents / actors (whether human or not) so that they can be tasked with automating repetitive tasks, mediating and fusing heterogeous data, and management of large virtual data repositories.

- *Providing Adaptive Resource Management.* Adaptive resource management enables dynamic adjustments (in all domains, including cyberspace) to be made to the relationships established between purposeful entities, including the ability to dynamically form groups / teams of appropriate sizes (so-called 'agile mission groupings' – see for example [Pynadath and Tambe 2003]). As circumstances change and services and entities come and go (owing to malicious or dysfunctional behaviour or failure or change of circumstances) then reconfiguration can occur without dislocation or catastrophic failure. This can be achieved by employing mechanisms such as domain and policy management.

5 Conclusion

Supporting military activity in is one of the most challenging tasks confronting democracies, but unfortunately, it is as important to address it effectively now as it has ever been. Enhanced information and decision support systems have been identified as critical to enabling our societies to effectively deal with the new military threats which currently confront them, and Agent Systems employing AAMAS technology are in our opinion one of the best candidates for providing these new systems. In this paper, we identified some of the issues which differentiate the task of constructing a system for use in the military domain from the task of system building in science and commerce, where to date Agent applications seem to have been most successful.

These issues included things such as :

- The need to overcome the organizational structures particular to the western military
- The particular operational environment of computing systems on the battle field
- The need to embrace uncertainty, complexity and heterogeneity
- The need to understand the adversarial nature of military operations
- The need to recognize the primacy of the human in military affairs.

We would recommend consideration of these issues to anyone thinking of employing multi-agent systems in the military domain. Our future activities in this area should drill down and map mature agent technologies that can address gaps in military information systems and identify emerging agent technologies that promise to significantly improve the desired properties outlined in this paper.

Acknowledgement

This paper was developed as the result of the numerous interactions that took place with many individuals associated with the defence community at AAMAS 2005, and afterwards. The authors of the paper wish to acknowledge their contribution and to thank them for their help.

References

1. D.S. Alberts, R. E. Hayes. "Power To the Edge. Command... Control... in the Information Age" CCRP, 2003.
2. D.N. Allsopp, P. Beautement, J.M Bradshaw, E.H. Durfee, M. Kirton, C.A. Knoblock, N. Suri, A. Tate, C.Q. Thompson. "Coalition Agents Experiment: Multiagent Cooperation in International Coalitions" IEEE Intelligent Systems, May/June 2002
3. M. Atighetchi, P. Pal, F. Webber, R. Schantz, C. Jones, J. Loyall (2004) "Adaptive Cyberdefense for Survival and Intrusion Tolerance," IEEE Internet Computing, vol. 08, no. 6, pp. 25-33, November/December, 2004.
4. J.M Bradshaw, P. Beautement, M.R. Breedy, L. Bunch, S.V. Drakunov, P. Feltovich, R. R. Hoffman, R. Jeffers, M. Johnson, S. Kulkarni, J. Lott, A.K. Raj, N. Suri, & A. Uszok "Making Agents Acceptable to People". In N. Zhong and J. Liu (Eds.), Handbook of Intelligent Information Technology. Amsterdam: IOS Press / Springer, 2004.
5. J.C. Bates (2005) UltraLog: Securing Logistics Information on the Battlefield, Army Logistician, Volume 37 (2) March-April 2005. U.S. Government Printing Office ISSN 0004-2528
6. V. Gorodetski, I. Kotenko (2002) "The Multi-agent Systems for Computer Network Security Assurance: Frameworks and Case Studies" Proceedings of the 2002 IEEE International Conference on Artificial Intelligence Systems (ICAIS'02), Geelong,Australia,February 12-15,2002

7. Hasard (2000) Written answers (Hoon) Debate of The United Kingdom Parliament 15th May 2000.

8. C. Hoile, F Wang, E Bonsma, P Marrow. (2002) "Core Specification and Experiments in DIET: A Decentralised Ecosystem-inspired Mobile Agent System", In Proceedings : Castelfranchi, C. & Johnson, W.L (eds.) First International Conference on Autonomous Agents and Multi-Agent Systems, pp 623 – 630. Bologna, Italy July 15-19th 2002.

9. J. Hollan, E. Hutchins & D. Kirsh, "Distributed cognition: Toward a new Foundation for Human-computer Interaction Research". University of California, San Diego. 2000.

10. Helsinger & T. Wright (2005) "Cougaar: A Robust Configurable Multi-Agent Platform" Submitted to IEEE Aerospace Conference 2005, BBN Technologies, Cambridge MA.

11. N.R. Jennings and M.J. Wooldridge (1998) Applications of Intelligent Agents. In: N.R. Jennings and M.J. Wooldridge (Eds.), Agent Technology Foundations, Applications and Markets. Springer-Verlag 1998.

12. D.V. Pynasath & M. Tambe "An Automated Teamwork Infrastructure for Hetrogeneous Software Agents and Humans". JAAMAS (Journal of Autonomous Agents and Multi-Agent Systems) 7:71—100, 2003.

13. Kotenko (2003) "Active Vulnerability Assessment of Computer Networks by Simulation of Complex Remote Attacks". Proceedings of the 2003 International Conference on Computer Networks and Mobile Computing (ICCNMC'03) Shanghai, China October 20-23, 2003.

14. Lakshmi Sandhana (2002) "The Drone Armies are Coming" Wired News, August 30th 2002.

15. T.E. Potok, L. Phillips, R. Pollock, A. Loebl and F. T. Sheldon (2003), "Suitability of Agent Technology for Command and Control in Fault-tolerant, Safety-critical Responsive Decision Networks" Proc.16th Int'l Conf. Parallel and Distributed Computing Systems, Reno NV, Aug. 13-15, 2003

16. N. Shadbolt, F. Ciravegna, J Domingue, W Hall, E Motta, K O'Hara, D Robertson, D Sleemean, A Tate, Y Wilks. (2004) "Advanced Knowledge Technologies at the Midterm: Tools and Methods for the Semantic Web" . In: N. Shadbolt, K, O'Hara (Eds.) Advanced Knowledge Technologies, Selected Papers 2004. AKT, UK 2004. ISBN 85432 8122

17. D. Talbot. (2004) "How Technology Failed in Iraq" MIT Technology Review, November 2004, http://www.technologyreview.com/articles/04/11/talbot1104.asp.

18. F.Wang, F.Gong, C. Sargor, K. Goseva-Popsto janova, K. Trivedi, F.Jou (2001) "SITAR: A Scalable Intrusion-Tolerant Architecture for Distributed Services" Proceedings of the 2001 IEEE Workshop on Information Assurance and Security T1B3 1100 United States Military Academy, West Point, NY, 5–6 June 2001

Enhanced Maritime Situation Awareness
with Negotiator Agents

Miniar Hemaissia[1], Amal El Fallah Seghrouchni[2], and Juliette Mattioli[1]

[1] THALES Research & Technology France, PLATON Lab,
RD 128, F-91767 Palaiseau Cedex, France
{miniar.hemaissia, juliette.mattioli}@thalesgroup.com
http://www.thalesgroup.com
[2] Université Paris 6, Laboratoire d'Informatique de Paris 6, UMR 7606 - CNRS,
8 rue du Capitaine Scott, F-75015 Paris, France
Amal.Elfallah@lip6.fr

Abstract. French coastguard missions have become increasingly varied implying new challenges such as the reduction of the decision cycle and the expansion of available information. Thus, it involves new needs for enhanced decision support. An efficient situation awareness system has to quickly detect and identify suspicious boats. The efficiency of such a system relies on a reliable sensor fusion since a coastguard uses sensors to achieve his mission. We present an innovative approach based on multi-agent negotiation to fuse classifiers, benefiting from the efficiency of existing classification tools and from the flexibility and reliability of a multi-agent system to exploit distributed data across dispersed sources. We developed a first prototype using a basic negotiation protocol in order to validate the feasibility and the interest of our approach. The results obtained are promising and encourage us to continue on this way.

1 Situation Awareness Challenge for a Maritime Supervision System

In France, maritime security is provided by regional operational monitoring and rescue centres called CROSS[1]. They are in charge of the surveillance and rescue coordination, navigation safety, traffic and pollution surveillance, coordination of fishing police missions and fishing effort control, etc. This operational organisation depends on the cooperation of the entire sea, air and land branches of maritime authorities such as the coastguard[2], national navy, customs and maritime Affairs. In addition, responding to CROSS entreaties, the coastguard operates national defence and general police in sea missions including looking for

---

[1] Centres Régionaux Opérationnels de Surveillance et de Sauvetage. Although a CROSS centre is a civil entity, it is mainly composed of military staff and equipments to carry out their missions.

[2] In France, the coastguard is a specialized branch of the national Gendarmerie, filling missions for the benefit of the Chief of Staff of the navy.

S.G. Thompson and R. Ghanea-Hercock (Eds.): DAMAS 2005 , LNAI 3890, pp. 14–23, 2006.
© Springer-Verlag Berlin Heidelberg 2006

and recording breach of laws, decrees and regulations, restoring and maintaining law and order, and also participating in operations concerning traffic protection, rescue and assistance of people in danger.

Therefore, coastguard missions have become increasingly varied such as responses to boat people, maritime pollution, and fish poaching; and a coastguard officer must maintain a general awareness of the supervised sea zone, yet focus on relevant contextual information when making decisions, without distraction from peripheral events in an ever-changing, uncertain environment. Decision cycles have shortened and available information has expanded. To meet these challenges, the officer needs enhanced decision support. Yet providing this automation becomes increasingly difficult as uncertainty increases. While the volume of raw information available to make decision at all levels is rapidly increasing, its coordination and dissemination as useful information becomes far more difficult, leading to "information overload". Data is often fragmented, uncertain, and distributed across different sources.

To address these issues, an efficient situation awareness system must provide information about the status, attributes and dynamics of relevant elements at sea (such as fishing boats, vessels, yachts, battleships, oil slicks, . . .). It also needs to include the classification of information, providing the basic building blocks for comprehension of the current situation. This comprehension encompasses how supervisor agents combine and interpret information. Thus, it includes more than perceiving or processing to information; it includes the integration of multiple pieces of information and a determination of their relevance to the underlying goals: target detection and identification. Situation Awareness is understood as a complex system composed of a set of semi-autonomous objects, physical (e.g. boat) or abstract (e.g. a software component in which the shape of a boat can be handled), having certain goals and operating to achieve a common goal. Recall that information is collected by different sources at different times. Situation is a notion of a dynamic nature and that is why input information may have different time stamps. As a rule, objects have different dynamics and therefore components of the collected information have different life times. Combining such information is a theoretical issue. Up to now, each type of information (signal, image, data base, . . .) has been processed on the basis of an appropriate and distinct approach.

Therefore, for future maritime supervision systems, an in-depth understanding of the officer cognitive processes must be achieved, coupled with innovative approaches for real-time information fusion at all levels, including multimedia and multi-modal information from different distributed sources that include huge amounts of uncertainty and noise. Such cognitively congruent systems will provide an intuitively understandable common operational picture for enhanced situation awareness. Our hypothesis is that the way to address the issues of information fusion at different levels is through negotiator agents that operate on classifiers outputs in order to detect and identify suspicious boats.

This paper presents our approach based on multi-agent systems and classifier fusion. It gives the modelling of our problem in a multi-agent system. A description of our prototype architecture follows, before giving an overview of its implementation and initial results. In section 6, a short overview of related work is presented. Finally, we conclude and propose the key issues for further research to design an efficient system for the identification problem.

2   Our Approach

In our application, to identify suspicious boats, the coastguard has several sensors available. These sensors are distributed and according to the sensor type, produced data are used to obtain different environmental information. To accommodate our identification requirements, different classification tools are developed in parallel, processing each information source enabling a coastguard officer to make a decision with the system support proposing possible solutions. There is a potential benefit to be gained by combining the results of different classification tools to maximize the advantages of each one while at the same time minimizing the disadvantages. This fusion scheme promises to deliver a result that is more accurate than the best possible result of any one tool employed. A number of methods have been developed for classifier fusion, essentially, there are two general groups of classifier fusion techniques [1]. The first group corresponds to methods operating on classifiers, emphasising on a development of the classifier structure to find a single best classifier or a selected group of classifiers and, only then, are their outputs taken as a final decision or for further processing. The other group consists of methods operating mainly on classifiers outputs, where the combination of classifiers outputs is calculated. Since classifications obtained are considered reliable enough, this second group of fusion methods was chosen.

Since sensors are distributed and a classifier is linked to a sensor, the use of a Multi-Agent System (MAS) seems to be a reliable method to exploit distributed data across different sources as in the case of distributed decision making process. Indeed, a MAS is a suitable answer when the solution has to combine, at least, distribution features and reasoning capabilities. An other motivation for using MAS lies in the fact that voting, and more generally automated negotiation, is considered as a classifier fusion method based on classifier outputs. MAS is well known to facilitate such negotiation at the operative decision making level. Therefore, our work focuses on using a multi-agent negotiation to do classifier fusion for an identification problem.

3   Agentification

How the problem is transposed in a MAS problem is a very important aspect when designing such a system. The agentification has an influence upon the systems efficiency in solving the problem. It turns out that the way to agentify a problem is a question of methodology. Therefore, in this section, we describe the elements and constraints taken into account in the modelling and the model itself.

Sensor functions can not be factorized or decomposed in our problem because we are not allowed to modify the sensors. Therefore, the agentification corresponds, at most, to the physical aspect: an agent represents a sensor. Nevertheless, some sensors can be switched over several modes. Each mode is independent from the others and a sensor operates in one mode at a time. This specific working allows us to define an agent per sensor mode, when possible to do so. Thus, we have a classifier per sensor mode. The classification process corresponds to a classification-identification capability linked to information on the environment which is provided by a sensor. Furthermore, one sensor provides this information once per mode. Therefore, the classification process corresponds to an agent capability and so there is an agent per sensor or sensor-mode when the sensor has several modes. In addition, to fuse classifiers, an automated negotiation process is used so that agents are considered as negotiators. This implies a negotiation capability and, in particular, an ability to evaluate alternatives e.g. submitted solutions.

The allocation of the sensors is mission-dependent and predefined configurations exist according to the type and the objectives of the mission. The coastguard officer then defines the sensors to use and these sensors are allocated to coastguard analysts. A coastguard analyst manages at least one sensor. He assists the officer in his identification task by providing him with information and precisions, such as visual information. The officer can also ask analysts to modify some sensor parameters, such as the mode, the direction or simply an update. Since the identification is supported by the officer as well as by the analysts, a classifier fusion occurs at the analyst's level and then the officer makes a decision. Accordingly, the negotiation process intervenes between the analysts, the experts on their sensors. In this context, the officer plays the role of negotiation initiator considering that he manages the overall process of identification but doesn't directly deal with sensors.

The modelling is based on the concepts of agent-group-role defined in the methodology Aalaadin [2]: a group is composed of several agents and an agent can belong to several groups; a role represents a function, a service or an identification of an agent in a particular group and each agent can be endowed with several roles. This methodology enables us to represent the effective organisation of the coastguard identification process. Figure 1 illustrates the agent model according to this methodology. The group structure identifies the overall roles and interactions in a group and the organisational structure specifies the problem in a general way. We decided to form groups according to the mission stages in the identification problem beginning with the mission configuration through to the identification itself. Therefore, a *configuration group* is defined with the following roles:

- Officer role, identifying the coastguard officer who manages and creates, in a way, the sensor manager but also sensors to be managed by himself;
- Sensor manager role, identifying the analyst who "creates", in turn, the sensors to be managed, and manages them;
- Sensor role to identify a sensor.

The classification task is represented in the *classification group* where there are:

- Analyst role, to identify the analyst who will receive sensor classifications;
- Classifier role for the classification function and to provide the results to the analyst.

And finally, the *negotiation group* is composed of:

- Initiator role, to initiate the negotiation, providing alternatives to the negotiators in order to get an identification;
- Negotiator role, the negotiation function.

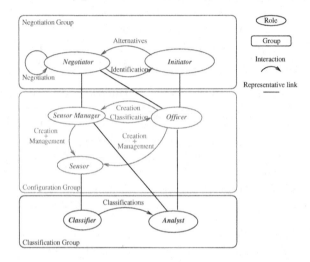

Fig. 1. Organisational structure of the identification problem. A *Representative* link joins two roles and corresponds to an agent that will have these roles.

Furthermore, in Fig. 1, there are representatives as specified in the Aalaadin methodology. These representatives identify the agents of our problem, linking the roles characterizing an agent. Thus, we have three types of agents:

1. Officer agent with the officer and the initiator roles. In addition to these roles, the officer agent can have the analyst role since the coastguard officer can manage sensors and so, assumes the roles of the analyst and the negotiator;
2. Analyst agent with the analyst, the sensor manager and the negotiator roles;
3. Sensor agent with the sensor and the classifier roles.

Therefore, our agentification follows the identification mechanism used by the coastguard. Actually, we represent the various actors as agents performing their roles. The agent representing a sensor acquires information, the processing of which provides a classification of possible identifications. The others agents are, first, the officer, defining the mission configuration, i.e. the sensors to be used, initiating the negotiation in order to determine the final classification or identification and also able to manage sensors and to negotiate, and, second, the analysts, managing sensors, recovering their classification and negotiating.

4   Architecture

Our agents are autonomous and intelligent entities and they also have some
mental components such as knowledge, capabilities and goals. To be more precise,
our agents' components are as defined in CLAIM language [3]:

- *knowledge* to represent information on the other agents or on the agent's
  environment (his world);
- *goals*, the agent's objectives;
- *messages*, a queue for storing arrived messages;
- *capabilities*, the agent's actions he can perform to achieve his goals or he can
  offer to an other agent;
- *processes* to represent the agent's processes executed in parallel;
- *parent* and *agents* to represent a hierarchical relationship. Indeed, a MAS
  CLAIM is a hierarchy of agents. Thus, an agent's parent is his creator and
  an agent's (sub-)agents are the agents he created.

Actually, a *processes* component is required since a sensor agent processes data to
provide environmental information in parallel to its classification task. Moreover,
an agent may create new agents. Dynamic creation of the agents is useful in
our application. For instance, the officer may create a team according to the
configuration of his mission. This implies a kind of hierarchy between the agents
in the system such as a "parent-child" relationship. Furthermore, the agents
communicate with each other to exchange information, to appeal a capacity and
so on. Consequently, we choose a message-passing communication which requires
a *messages* component.

Since sensors have a permanent task of analysing the environment, our agents
need processes to be executed in parallel to the classification task. This last

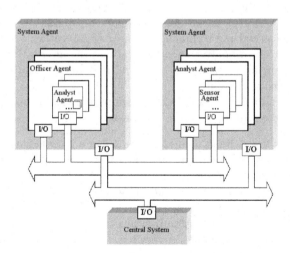

Fig. 2. The system architecture

property requires us to take into account the mobility aspect of the agent. Indeed, if the computation is large, it could be useful to be able to dispatch the load over several machines. Figure 2 shows the system architecture which is inspired by the SyMPA architecture [4].

5   Implementation and Initial Results

A prototype based on the system architecture described above has been developed with the Himalaya framework [4]. This framework is composed of the SyMPA platform and supports the Claim language as an agent oriented programming language. We defined three classes of agents: officer, analyst and sensor. These agent classes implement the agents' components described in section 4. In particular, there are the capabilities required in the agent model described in section 3:

1. Officer agent class capabilities:
   (a) *createTeam*: enables an officer agent to create a team according to the mission configuration enabling the officer agent to play his *officer role*. Note, a team is defined giving the analyst list to create with the sensor types they will manage;
   (b) *proposeAlternatives*: enables the officer agent to play his initiation role, providing alternatives to the analysts in his team;
   (c) *solve*: since a voting protocol is used, the officer agent applies the election rules defined by the chosen protocol to get an identification according to the votes of the analysts;
2. Analyst agent class capabilities:
   (a) *createSensor*: enables an analyst agent to create the sensors the analyst will manage according to the types provided by the officer. This capability enables the analyst agent to play his sensor manager role;
   (b) *classification*: enables an analyst agent to provide his classification to the officer according to managed sensor classifications;
   (c) *vote*: enables an analyst agent to evaluate the alternatives given by the officer agent in order to vote, hence,to play his negotiator role;
3. Sensor agent class capability:
   (a) *classify*: enables a sensor agent to compute a classification according to the processed information on the observed target.

Other capabilities are defined to update the agent's knowledge such as sensors classifications or votes of the analysts. Moreover, the officer agent has a goal corresponding to getting an identification.

To start, in this prototype, an analyst agent will only manage one sensor at a time to simplify the problem: to avoid the fusion of the sensor classifiers and so to focusing on the negotiation between the analysts. Figure 3 presents an analyst and the sensor he manages. A very basic and simple negotiation protocol, a truthful voting protocol, is used. This protocol is the Borda protocol: each alternative is assigned a count based upon the agent's preferences on a list of O

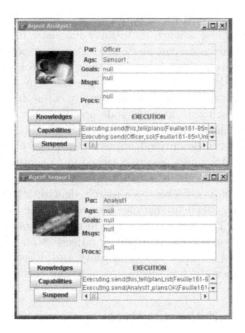

Fig. 3. Screen shot of part of the prototype: an analyst agent on top and the sensor he manages down below

alternatives, $|O|$ for the preferred alternative, $|O| - 1$ for the next one and so on. The counts are then summed for all agents, the winning alternative being the one with the highest score. Therefore, according to the sensor classifications, the analysts will give the Borda count to the officer. Then the officer will sum the scores and obtain an identification for the observed target.

Preliminary tests have been realized using classifiers elaborated according to each sensor and with support from sensor operational experts. We tested about 20 scenarios with mission configuration using several sensor types and so sensor agents. The tests have been compared to the real target identity and we obtained an identity ranked 4th on average amongst more than 20 possible alternatives. Therefore, using a very basic and simple negotiation protocol, we obtained reasonable results although they are not acceptable for our application. Nevertheless, the use of more sophisticated protocols should enable us to obtain much better results, hence, a much more efficient system.

6   Related Work

Many works on sensor fusion exists but only few of them use MAS or a decentralized method to fuse sensor information. In [5], a meta-classifier uses the results of classifications produced by other classifiers in a MAS to fuse information. The agents defined are not representing data sources but several entities with specialized roles and cooperating to perform the information fusion. In [6], the sensor fusion is performed using a multi-layer linguistic inference method and the agents give a local decision considering an agent is an expert capable of lower level fusion to suggest recommendations for the global decision-maker. An other approach based on a decentralized fusion is presented in [7]. This approach is based on a target identification algorithm for fully connected networks in which local target identity estimates at each node are directly calculated as either a posteriori probability distributions or Dempster-Shafer bodies of evidence. The most relevant work is the design and implementation of a target identification system based on a MAS where agents correspond to sensors and where sensor fusion is performed by a consensus method fusing classifiers linked to sensors [8]. The classifier fusion is achieved by a search algorithm based on a numerical method computing the euclidean distance between specific measures, in order to rank the alternatives. This work inspired us in the elaboration of our approach and prototype because of the similarity of our objectives and the efficiency of this system. However, SMA2 system lacks flexibility and doesn't take into account the interactions between the final decision-maker and the sensor managers.

7   Conclusion and Perspectives

For future maritime supervision systems, the development of systems supporting decision makers in maintaining a general awareness of the supervised zone is a key issue. In particular, since an officer is facing a large amount of information and a shorter time to decide, the support system must provide the most relevant information available. To propose a solution to this problem, we presented an approach focused on sensor information fusion. The aim is to combine the benefits and efficiency of existing classification tools. Moreover, since sensors are distributed entities and the appropriate classifier depends on the sensors, we combined fusion and MAS. Therefore, using a negotiation protocol as a fusion tool in a MAS, we obtained a flexible system: the negotiation protocol is a parameter of the system. The results we obtained with a very simple negotiation protocol encourages us to continue in this direction. Indeed, the identifications we obtained are not so far from the real identity of the target. Therefore, to design an efficient system for this identification problem, the next steps of our study are, first, to improve the negotiation protocol taking into account information available on sensor classifications and, second, to deal with the management of several sensors by an analyst, taking into account the dependencies between sensor and/or analyst's information.

Acknowledgements

We wish to thank Gabriel Marchalot and Gilles Coppin for their availability and their support, in particular for putting SMA2 at our disposal, and Alexandru Suna for the Himalaya Framework.

References

1. Ruta, D., Gabrys, B.: An overview of classifier fusion methods. Computing and Information Systems **7** (2000) 1–10
2. Ferber, J., Gutknecht, O.: A meta-model for the analysis and design of organizations in multi-agent systems. In: Third International Conference on Multi-Agent Systems, ICMAS98. (1998) 128–135
3. El Fallah-Seghrouchni, A., Suna, A.: Claim: A computational language for autonomous, intelligent and mobile agents. In: Programming Multiagent Systems. Volume 3067 of LNAI., Springer (2004)
4. El Fallah-Seghrouchni, A., Suna, A.: Himalaya framework: Hierarchical intelligent mobile agents for building large-scale and adaptive systems based on ambients. In: International Workshop on Massively Multi-Agent Systems, Kyoto, Japan (2004)
5. Gorodetsky, V., Karsaev, O., Kotenko, I., Samoilov, V.: Multi-agent information fusion: methodology, architecture and software tool for learning of object and situation assessment. In: Seventh International Conference on Information Fusion (Fusion 04), Stockholm, Sweden (2004) 346–353
6. Chen, T.M., Luo, R.C.: Multilevel multiagent based team decision fusion for autonomous tracking system. International Journal on Machine Intelligence and Robotic Control **1** (2000) 489–494
7. Oxenham, M.G., Challa, S., Morelande, M.R.: Decentralised fusion of disparate identity estimates for shared situation awareness. In: Seventh International Conference on Information Fusion (Fusion 04), Stockholm, Sweden (2004) 167–174
8. SMA2 Consortium: Rapport de synthèse finale. A french project, SMA2 Consortium (2003)

Agent-Based Parsimonious Decision Support Paradigm Employing Bayesian Belief Networks

Panos Louvieris, Andreas Gregoriades, Natasha Mashanovich, Gareth White, Robert O'Keefe, Jerry Levine1, and Stewart Henderson

Surrey Defence Technology Centre, University of Surrey, UK
{panos.louvieris, a.gregoriades, n.mashanovich,
g.white, r.o'keefe}@surrey.ac.uk
C2DC, Land Warfare Centre, Warminster, UK
c2dc@milnet.uk.net

Abstract. This paper outlines the application of Bayesian technologies to CSF (Critical Success Factor) assessment for parsimonious military decision making using an agent-based decision support system. The research referred to in this paper is part of a funded project concerned with Smart Decision Support Systems (SDSS) within the General Dynamics led Data and Information Fusion Defence Technology Centre Consortium in the UK. An important factor for successful military missions is information superiority (IS). However, IS is not solely about minimising information related needs to avoid information overload and the reduction of bandwidth. It is concerned with creating information related capabilities that are aligned with achieving operational effects and raising operational tempo. Moreover good military decision making, agent based or otherwise, should take into account the uncertainty inherent in operational situations. While efficient information fusion may be achieved through the deployment of CSFs, Bayesian Belief Networks (BBNs) are employed to model uncertainty. This paper illustrates the application of CSF enabled BBN technology through an agent based paradigm for assessing the likelihood of success of military missions. BBNs are composed of two parts the quantitative and the qualitative. The former models the dependencies between the various random events and the latter the prior domain knowledge embedded in the network in the form of conditional probability tables (CPTs). Modelling prior knowledge in a BBN is a complex and time consuming task and sometimes intractable when the number of nodes and states of the network increases. This paper describes a method that enables the automated configuration of conditional probability tables from hard data generated from simulations of military operational scenarios using a computer generated forces (CGF) synthetic environment.

1 Introduction

In complex domains such as warfighting, military decisions need to be made based on up to date, relevant and timely information. Failing to acquire relevant, timely and reliable information reduces the likelihood of success. Information however could

S.G. Thompson and R. Ghanea-Hercock (Eds.): DAMAS 2006, LNCS 3890, pp. 24–36, 2006.
© Springer-Verlag Berlin Heidelberg 2006

become a burden if it is supplied uncontrolled, in large quantities. Therefore it is important to be able to fuse and process relevant information efficiently through automation. Automation can be used at each stage of the process, from the acquisition, fusion to the processing. Our aim in this paper is to focus on the processing of information in order to assist the decision maker. For this task we employ a decision theoretic approach named Bayesian Belief Network. The correctness of the reasoning made with BBNs is analogous to the quality of knowledge that they encapsulate. Therefore, it is important that the knowledge that is incorporated in the BBN model evolves at the same pace as the domain that is modelled. This requires a continuous learning process which can be achieved through machine learning.

Information in the military domain is characterised by many uncertainties that should be modelled in order to maximise effectiveness. BBN is a mature method applied in numerous domains where uncertainty is a predominating factor [4]. In recent years BBNs have become increasingly recognised as a potentially powerful solution to complex risk assessment problems [4]. Because uncertainty is a property that characterises many domains, BBN technology has become very popular. Example applications include decision support, medical diagnostics, troubleshooting, risk analysis, safety assessment and image processing.

However despite their many advantages BBNs suffer from one major disadvantage, the modelling of prior domain knowledge as conditional probability distributions. This problem lies in the heart of Bayesian probability theory. The number of probability distributions required to populate a conditional probability table (CPT) grows exponentially with the number of nodes involved [2][3]. In the absence of hard data, we must rely on domain experts to provide, often subjective judgements to inform the CPT. However, if the table is to be populated through knowledge elicited from a domain expert then the sheer magnitude of the task forms a considerable cognitive barrier. For instance, consider a model that has two parent nodes which converge to a third child node in a Y shape; and, if each node has five states ranging from very low to very high then the CPT for the child node would have 125 states. This is not an impossible number to elicit but due to experts biases inconsistencies will arise. If the number of states increases to seven then the elicitation becomes impracticable. The problem and challenge is not new. It has been addressed by Druzdzel [2], Takikawa [13] and Wellman [14]. Approaches exist that attempt to reduce the complexity of the problem such as Noisy-OR model proposed by Pearl [9]. However this approach assumes that the parent nodes are conditionally independent of each other and there is negligible inter-parent influence towards the child node. Lemmer and Gossink [5] advanced the Noisy-OR approach by overcoming the independence requirement among parents. However their approach is restricted only to binary nodes (only two states). Alternative approaches concentrate on minimising the effort required by domain experts. Our approach, based on statistical measures, inductively calculates the conditional probabilities from hard data that is obtained from CGF simulations of military scenarios. This paper is organised in four sections. Initially we introduce the notion of uncertainty through BBNs and their application to CSF assessment, the underlying concepts of military decision making are illustrated, the architecture of a system employing the approach is explained and finally the approach is described.

2 Military Decision Making

Commanders rely on the support of experienced, highly trained and capable staff officers in order to make informed decisions. Similarly for any smart DSS to be of real value, it must support commanders' intuitive decision making. Increasingly in the emerging NEC (Networked Enabled Capability) era, the use of artificial intelligence techniques in DSSs that fully integrate the human dimension will facilitate better informed decision making; ultimately, resulting in more timely and appropriate effects [10].

The primary aim in a decision making process is to reach the best available decision using timely, fused, pertinent and prioritised information well before the enemy with the minimum resources. In order to achieve this, modern decision making processes integrate human and machine capabilities to improve efficiency and effectiveness. Our approach integrates military domain expertise with a powerful reasoning technique (BBN) to assist commanders in achieving the intended outcome with reliable, efficient and timely supply of information. Information dominance/ superiority however is characterised by the superior generation, manipulation and use of information [8]. Timeliness is critical. Information is gathered about an enemy in a given set of circumstances. The friendly commander will make his plan based on the enemy's activities and must execute it before the situation changes to the extent that his plan becomes increasingly inappropriate and is eventually invalidated. Therefore it is important for an automated system that assists this task to incorporate up-to-date information regarding the domain. Such a system should include military domain knowledge that evolves in accordance to the domain that it models. Manually updating the encapsulated knowledge in the BBN model is unrealistic. As a result we employ a CGF simulation tool, i.e. VR-Forces, in accordance with a training agent that automatically configures the model with the required knowledge based on data generated via simulation.

Key to the whole process is understanding the needs of the customer. 'Customer buy-in' is essential to imbuing potential users - the commander - with trust in the system such that it is perceived as a useful decision support tool to whose development he is willing to contribute and encourage his subordinates to the same. Subject Matter Experts (SMEs) in the warfighting domain are key to informing our investigation and numerous SME workshops continue to enhance our knowledge to this process. Our SME workshops and subsequent analysis revealed the critical information requirements considered essential for commanders during the decision making process. These fused information requirements, which constitute the CSFs, are fundamental to determining the CSFs' state for a mission, and need to be monitored constantly throughout the execution of a military scenario [6][11]. BBN technology is employed to model the uncertainties influencing the CSFs. Findings from the initial domain analysis were used to construct the BBN networks to assess the CSFs. In this paper BBN technology is employed to assess a single CSF, i.e. Relative Strength, to illustrate the concept.

3 Uncertainty Modelling with Bayesian Belief Networks

Uncertainty has been an integral part of every complex system. In the early days due to the constraints of early probability modelling which required either the specification of intractable number of parameters or the assumption of unrealistic set of independence relationships among influences, it was impossible to apply it in any realistic problems. Recently, due to the advances in uncertainly modelling with the support of graphical modelling and powerful inference algorithms that managed to overcome the computational complexities involved, decision makers are able to use probability theory in their systems by incorporating qualitative and quantitative information in a single model.

Bayesian belief networks are an established methodology that enable the modelling of uncertainty. It has recently gained widespread use due to the introduce- tion of powerful algorithms that enabled the exploitation of their capabilities [9]. A Bayesian network is a directed acyclic graph that describes probabilistic relationships among random variables of interest. The representation rigorously describes these relationships, through a human oriented qualitative structure that facilitates communication comprehensibility by users and a quantitative part incorporating the probabilistic model. Probabilistic inference can be performed using the BBN model to predict the outcome of variables based on the observations of others. The next section illustrates the BBN model used to assess a single critical success factor, named Relative Strength.

4   BBN Model for Relative Strength Assessment

Based on the influencing factors identified through domain analysis we developed a set of BBN models to assess a number of CSFs. The BBN model that assesses the probability that Relative Strength is satisfactory/adequate/unsatisfactory is illustrated here. The qualitative part of this model is depicted in fig 1. Each node corresponds to a random variable and is described by a number of states that the variable could have. Arcs between the various nodes define the relationships between the variables (dependencies). These arcs never form cycles between nodes in order to comply with the underline principles of probability theory. Therefore these are called directed acyclic graphs DAGs.

BBN strength resides in the integration of the qualitative with the quantitative parts. Therefore as already stated we need to populate the CPT of Table 1 based on SME knowledge. Each random variable depicted as a node in the model, is described by the conditional probability function of that variable given the parents in the graph, i.e., the collection of conditional probability functions {f(xi | pa (xi))}. The underlying assumptions of conditional independence encoded in the graph allow us to calculate the joint probability function using equation (1):

$$p(x_1,...,x_{i-1}) = \prod_{i=1}^{n} p(x_i|x_1,...,x_{i-1})$$
(1)

The next section explains how this BBN is trained with hard data obtained from simulations before it is employed to predict the status of the required information.

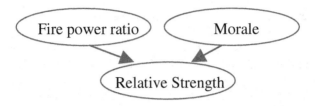

Fig. 1. Qualitative representation of BBN that assesses relative strength

Table 1. Quantitative representation of a BBN that assesses relative strength

		FPR=Good			FPR=Average			FPR=Bad		
		M= H	M= M	M= L	M= H	M= M	M= L	M= H	M= M	M= L
Relati ve Strength (RS)	Satisfactory									
	Adequate									
	~Satisfact ory									

5   Learning Bayesian Belief Networks

Learning is necessary in domains that are constantly evolving. In order to make effective decisions using BBNs, it is important to incorporate in the model the most up-to-date knowledge. Knowledge in BBN is represented in both the qualitative and the quantitative parts of the model. The qualitative part corresponds to medium to long term changes in the domain while the quantitative to short term changes. Our focus in this paper is in the evolution of the quantitative part of the model which represents the CPTs of the model. Population of the CPTs however is difficult. When the networks are small it is possible to consult SMEs to define the CPT values. However this is not an easy task since domain experts are difficult to find and most of the times they do not reach a consensus due to bias and preoccupations. This presents a challenge. 'Customer buy-in' can be reinforced if parameters of learning are sufficiently bounded to ensure a high degree of confidence in the veracity of the learning. This implies the need for a vast number of 'learning experiences' in order to produce a reliable process, which in turn ideally requires input from many SMEs with as close a consensus as possible; hence the use of scenarios or vignettes which are most likely to achieve consensus in a given population of SMEs.

In order to overcome the problem of SME subjective bias, the requirement for automated CPT population either from data is obvious. In the case that the data is available and the structure of the network is known then the CPTs can be populated using a number of candidate approaches such as machine learning, statistical techniques or data mining. In the case that the data is incomplete but the structure of the network is known the problem becomes a bit more complex since it is necessary to predict from incomplete data for all variables the probability distributions for all variables. There are numerous approaches for achieving this. One of the most popular is Expectancy Maximisation (EM) algorithm [1]. In our case we have complete data that is generated from a CGF synthetic environment and the structure of the BBN is derived from initial domain analysis (CSF influences). A detailed description of the approach is described the following section.

6 Agent Based Learning

The purpose of the learning agent is to train the BBN models based on simulations of past military scenarios (fig 2). To achieve this we employ a CGF tool named VR-Forces, which is a powerful and flexible simulation software product for generating and executing battlefield scenarios [7]. It provides all the necessary simulation to be used as a tactical leadership trainer, threat generator, behaviour model test-bed, or Computer Generated Forces (CGF) application. Throughout simulation of each operational scenario we monitor (using the tool's API) the parameters that are important for achieving the overall objective of a mission. These were identified through domain analysis and constitute the influences to the critical success factors of each scenario. In this paper we concentrate on relative strength of the friendly units. The main influences to relative strength are fire power ratio and relative morale. The former can be obtained from VR-Forces by monitoring the fire power of the friendly and enemy units and subsequently calculating the ratio by using the following equation:

$$FPR = \frac{Friendly\_Fire\_Power}{Enemy\_Fire\_Power} \tag{2}$$

Relative morale corresponds to the ratio between the friendly and enemy's forces morale. This is an SME specified subjective measure and is entered into the system manually for each scenario. In the deployed system, this might represent the need for the application of the commander's military judgement on a qualitative factor to a scenario which has insufficient data available to give a trustworthy indication, in which the commander can believe. After simulating the various scenarios and obtaining the required data the training agent inductively generates the CPTs of each of the BBN models. The trained BBN models are subsequently used by the reasoning agent during execution mode (real operations or war gaming) to assess the

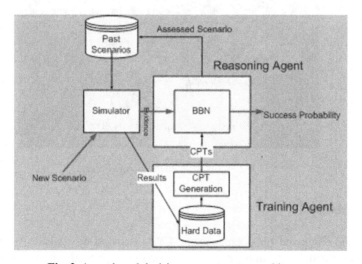

Fig. 2. Agent based decision support system architecture

probability of each CSF being satisfactory. Evidences obtained from observations during the simulation of a scenario in VR-forces (fig 2) are propagated down the BBN models to give rise to the probability of success.

7 Scenario of Use

The scenario employed to illustrate the approach is a land-based "Breach" scenario. The intent of the friendly units is to clear a minefield prior to destroying a target. In order to achieve this, a number of armed friendly vehicles firstly attack the enemy armed vehicles which are guarding the minefield. When this is achieved the mine clearance vehicle proceeds and creates a path from which the friendly units can pass. A diagrammatic representation of the scenario is shown in fig 3 using VR-Forces. Square shape entities correspond to friendly armed vehicles and diamond shape entities to enemy armed vehicles. Friendly units on the left bottom corner are advancing towards the enemy units on the right top corner. The anti-tank minefield in between is represented with a doted rectangle. Single headed arrows describe the axis of attack and double headed arrows the main attack. During simulation the entities act semi-autonomously according to predefined Courses of Action specified in the scenario.

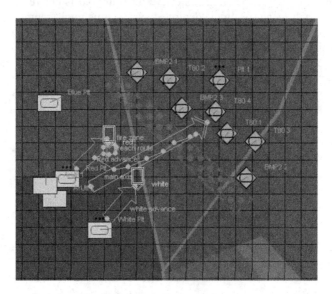

Fig. 3. Breach scenario in VR-Forces

8 The Method

The method employed for populating the CPTs is based on statistical measures on data obtained from the simulations. In this paper we are focus on the assessment of the "Relative Strength" CSF. This is influenced by two parameters the fire power ratio and relative morale determined through a series of SME workshops [12]. These two influences are collated into one equation for calculating relative strength, as shown below:

$$Relative\ Strength = FPR * Relative\ Morale \qquad (3)$$

To calculate the prior conditional probabilities of the CPT we use the data generated from the VR Forces scenario simulations. Initially we simulate a scenario using VR Forces a number of times with different variations. During each time step of the simulation we monitor the fire power of the friendly and enemy forces and calculate FPR (Fire Power Ratio). The graphical representation of this is shown in fig 3. Based on the FPR and in conjunction with a user defined setting of relative morale we calculate the relative strength based on equation (3). The result of this function is plotted and shown in fig 4. According to the level of granularity that we wish to model the problem, the analogous number of states are defined in the BBN nodes. The prior probabilities are calculated based on this number of permissible states and their associated thresholds. In this case the number of states for relative strength node are {"not satisfactory", "adequate" "satisfactory"}. For FPR is {"Good", "Medium", "Bad"} and relative morale is {"High", "Medium", "Low"}. Based on these we require two thresholds as depicted in fig 4. The number of observations above the threshold are used to calculate the probability that relative strength/FPR is in Satisfactory/Good states analogously in accordance with equation (4). Letter "N" represents the total number of observations obtained from the simulation of the

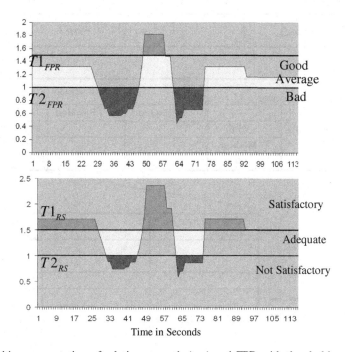

Fig. 4. Graphic representation of relative strength (top) and FPR with thresholds values and corresponding states

particular scenario. Likewise, the number of observations between thresholds one and two defines the probability of relative strength/FPR being in Adequate/Average states. Similarly for observations below threshold two define the probability of Relative strength/FPR being unsatisfactory/bad states.

$$P(FPR_{Good}) = \frac{\sum_{t=1}^{N} P(f_{FPR}(t) > T1_{FPR})}{N} \tag{4}$$

To calculate the prior probabilities of FPR we repeat the process with variations of the same scenario and calculate the frequencies as shown in Table 2.

To calculate the prior conditional probabilities of Relative Strength we repeat the process with different SME approved settings of relative morale for the same scenario. Relative Morale settings take values between [0,2]. Zero represents low relative morale (enemy's morale higher than own) and two equates to high relative morale. The results after thresholding the observations are collated in a matrix

Table 2. Prior probability distribution of FPR

FPR	Priors
Good	$P(f_{FPR}(t) > T1_{FPR})$
Average	$P(f_{FPR}(t) > T2_{FPR} - f_{FPR}(t) > T1_{FPR})$
Bad	$P(f_{FPR}(t) < T2_{FPR})$

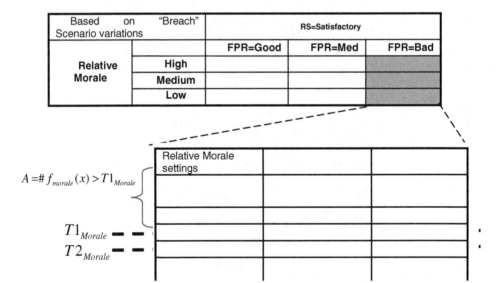

Fig. 5. Calculating prior conditional probabilities for Relative Strength CSF

Table 3. Collated results of initial probabilities for Relative Strength and FPR with various setting of Relative Morale

$f_{morale}(x)$	$P(f_{FPR}(t)<T2_{FPR})$	$P(f_{RS}(t)>T1_{RS})$	
2		0.30	
1.8		0.29	$\dfrac{0.3+0.29+0.28}{3}=0.29$
1.6		0.28	
1.4		0.27	
1.3		0.26	$\dfrac{0.27+0.26+0.25}{3}=0.26$
1.2		0.25	
0.9		0	
0.5		0	
0.2		0	

(Side labels: $T1_{Morale}$ indicated at the dashed line between 1.6 and 1.4; $T2_{Morale}$ indicated at the dashed line between 1.2 and 0.9)

depicted in fig 5. Based on these we can calculate the probability of relative strength being satisfactory given FPR is bad and relative morale is either high/medium/low. This corresponds to the third column of table 3. The process is repeated with variations of the same scenario were FPR is in medium and good states in order to calculate the probabilities for the remaining columns of the CPT table. For instance to calculate the prior conditional probability of relative strength being satisfactory given relative morale is high and FPR is bad using equation 5, we sum the probabilities of relative strength which are satisfactory based on relative morale settings which are above threshold one. The sum is divided by, A, the total number of scenario variations defined by the number of morale settings.

$$P(RS_{Sat} \mid Morale_{High}, FPR_{Bad}) == \frac{\sum P(f_{RS}(t)>T1_{RS})}{A} \qquad (5)$$

9   Results

After 12 simulations of the "Breach" scenario in VR-Forces the conditional probability distributions converged to their true value and that determined the end of the BBN training process. Analysing the data using the method described we obtained the results depicted in table 2. Averaging the probabilities of relative strength being in "Satisfactory" state based on relative morale settings above threshold one and FPR being low we can obtain the probability that relative strength is satisfactory. Analogously we can calculate the probability that relative strength is satisfactory given fire power is low and relative morale is accordingly medium and high. Table 4 illustrates the results obtained for part of the CPT.

Having trained the BBN with the data generated from the simulations it can be employed to predict the probability that relative strength is satisfactory at each time-step of a new scenario simulation. Therefore, during scenario execution the system monitors the fire power of friendly and enemy units, computes the fire power ratio and uses that as input evidence to the BBN. Relative morale setting is also used as input evidence. Both evidences are propagated down the network that returns the required probability distributions for relative strength.

Table 4. Results obtained for part of the CPT

| | | FPR=Low | | |
		Morale=High	Morale=Med	Morale=Low
Relative Strength	Satisfactory	$\frac{0.3 + 0.29 + 0.28}{3} = 0.29$	$\frac{0.27 + 0.26 + 0.25}{3} = 0.26$	0
	Adequate	0.17	0.12	0
	Not Satisfactory	0.54	0.62	1

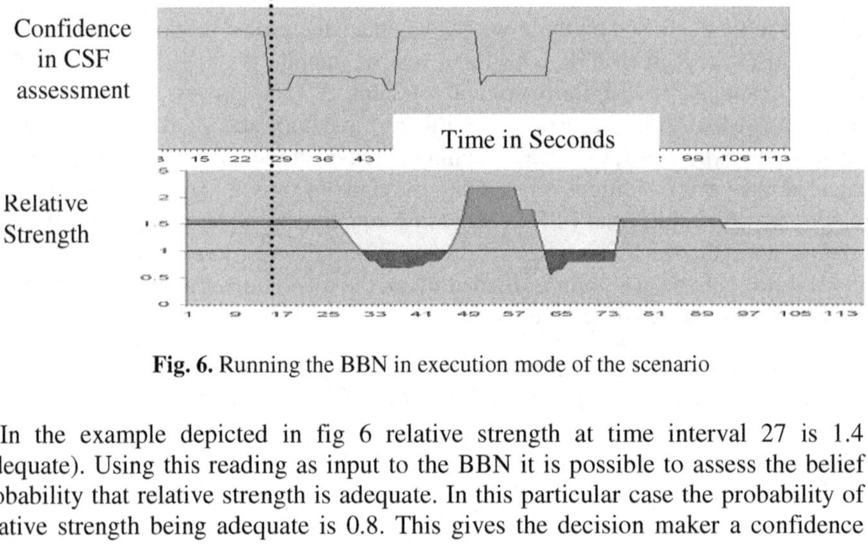

Fig. 6. Running the BBN in execution mode of the scenario

In the example depicted in fig 6 relative strength at time interval 27 is 1.4 (adequate). Using this reading as input to the BBN it is possible to assess the belief probability that relative strength is adequate. In this particular case the probability of relative strength being adequate is 0.8. This gives the decision maker a confidence measure of the calculated Relative Strength CSF.

10 Conclusions

This paper has outlined and reported on the preliminary findings of an approach to support the military decision making process intended to improve the effectiveness and efficiency of the decision maker i.e. the commander. The principle behind the approach is the automated assessment of CSFs that are important to achieving the mission objectives and effects. Automation is realised based on BBN and agent-based technologies. However, the difficulty of constructing the quantitative part of the

BBNs hinders their effectiveness. Our approach overcomes this limitation through a statistical analysis of simulated results obtained from the 'Breach' scenario. Further, it overcomes the issue of temporal discrepancies between scenarios when calculating prior probabilities. The data generated from the CGF simulations is used to construct inductively the CPTs through a training agent. The trained BBN is applied subsequently to assess the confidence in the calculation of the Relative Strength CSF during the execution mode of a new scenario. SME qualitative assessment suggests that the initial results from the method are encouraging. The advantage this approach is that it can generate variety of scenario results using the CGF simulator; hence provide a broad range of training data. The training process is completed when the generated CPT values converge [15]. Alternative approaches are often pathological to the data limitation problem which could lead to biased CPT population. Although an approximation, the CGF simulator nevertheless provides a useful bounded representation of reality for experimental purposes. Further experimentation and SME validation are required to confirm suitability and acceptability of this approach, and are scheduled in the project's research programme. Moreover, we are aiming to improve the technique by tackling situations in scenarios where the data is incomplete or missing.

Acknowledgements

We gratefully acknowledge the support of Col. Crispian Beattie, his officers and staff at C2DC Land Warfare Centre Warminster UK for facilitating and contributing to the workshops. Also, we acknowledge the support of General Dynamics (UK) and JSCSC staff in the workshop activities. *Panos Louvieris, Surrey Defence Technology Centre (Surrey DTC), is the principal investigator and lead for the Smart DSS project described herein. We thank DSTL/MoD for granting permission to publish this work.

References

1. Dempster, A. P., Laird, N. M., et al.: "Maximum Likelihood Estimation from Incomplete Data via the EM Algorithm.", Journal of the Royal Statistical Society, 39, 1-38, (1977)
2. Druzdzel, MK and van der Gaag L.C.: "Elicitation of probabilities for belief networks: combining qualitative and quantitative information", Proceedings 11th Annual Conference on Uncertainty in Artificial Intelligence (UAI-95), Montreal, Quebec, Canada, August, 141-148 (1995)
3. Druzdzel, M.K. and van der Gaag, L.C.: "Building Probabilistic Networks: Where Do the Numbers Come From?", IEEE Transactions on Knowledge and Data Engineering, 12(4) 481-486 (2000).
4. Heckerman, D., Mamdani A., Wellman M.: "Real-world applications of Bayesian networks", Communications of the ACM, 38(3), 25-26 (1995)
5. Lemmer, J. F and Gossink D. E.: Recursive noisy OR – A rule for estimating complex probabilistic interactions, IEEE Transactions on Systems, Man, and Cybernetics – Part B: Cybernetics, 43(5), 2252-2261 (2004)
6. Louvieris, P. and Beswick, P.: "Meeting the commander's information needs during the execution of a mission", British Army Review, , No.135, Autumn, 34-35 (2004)

7. MAK: VR-Forces, MAK technologies, (2005) www.mak.com
8. Miller, D.: Information dominance, "The philosophy of total propaganda control", Coldtype, (2004)
9. Pearl, J.: "Probabilistic Reasoning in Intelligent Systems: Network of Plausible Inference", Morgan Kaufmann Publishers: San Francisco, California, (1988)
10. MoD: Networked enabled capability, MoD, (2005)
11. Louvieris, P.: "Critical Success Factors: A Brief Account", Surrey DTC report, University of Surrey, UK (2004)
12. Louvieris, P. et al : "Scenarios Development and CSF Elicitation", No.2, Surrey DTC report, (2005)
13. Takikawa, M. and D'Ambrosio, B.: "Multiplicative Factorization of Noisy-Max", Proceedings of the Uncertainty in AI Conference , (1999)
14. Wellman, M.P.: "Fundamental concepts of qualitative probabilistic networks", Artificial Intelligence, 44(3), 257-303, (1990)
15. Buntine, W.: "A guide to the literature on learning probabilistic networks from data", IEEE Transactions on Knowledge and Data Engineering, 8(2), 195 – 210, (1996)

Distributed Decision-Making and Control
for Agile Military Radio Networks

James Wise, Gareth Smith, John Salt, Paul Huey, and Graham Atkins

General Dynamics United Kingdom Limited,
Bryn Brithdir, Oakdale Business Park, Oakdale, Blackwood, South Wales, NP12 4AA
{james.wise, gareth.smith, john.salt, paul.huey,
graham.atkins}@generaldynamics.uk.com

Abstract. We propose an agent-based autonomic network control system that allows an agile mission group to reconfigure their network, while maintaining a high tempo, yet minimise their demands on signals staff. Our architecture describes services that configure a device, and a hierarchy of networks, in terms of the contribution that each makes to networks of which it is a member, end-to-end services provided to its users, and objectives assigned to it by the signals staff. Agent-based services accept high-level direction from commanders, through signals staff, and cooperate to decide and enforce policies for the control of network configuration, services and traffic in support of the mission objectives and the changing needs of the users. To experiment with services that implement our architecture, we created a testbed that provides emulated terminals as part of an emulated military network that can replicate the end-to-end conditions present in a variety of wired and radio network environments.

1 Introduction

Agile mission groups are important to the conduct of military operations [1]. They rely on personnel and materiel that belong to different military units being able to form into a unified whole for the duration of a specific mission. Group members must be able to communicate and cooperate with one another while commanders need to command and control their subordinates and coordinate actions. They must also maintain a high tempo (rate of activity in relation to the enemy).

During a mission, the combination of constraints (including very low bandwidth channels, high mobility, zero (or minimal) infrastructure and a very adverse environment) and success criteria (completion of the mission irrespective of network performance per user) make this a particularly challenging application domain.

Current techniques require an off-line, manually-intensive process to plan a deployable network in detail ahead of use and then manage low-level automatic and manual configuration of network devices. This is a cumbersome process, ill-suited to address on-the-fly changes if unpredictable adverse events occur during the mission.

Against this background, we believe that an autonomic military radio network can provide significant advantages over a manually maintained network. Such a network can self-configure, given its mission objectives, and reconfigure on-the-fly to maintain those objectives while supporting its users as effectively as possible, given the dynamic constraints that it experiences during the execution of a mission.

S.G. Thompson and R. Ghanea-Hercock (Eds.): DAMAS 2005, LNAI 3890, pp. 37–50, 2006.
© Springer-Verlag Berlin Heidelberg 2006

We are adapting emerging techniques in the fields of multi-agent systems [6, 7, 12] and distributed network management [4, 11] to the creation of novel communication systems for the military radio networking domain that are agile, flexible and effective.

In particular, we believe that the nature of this domain will lead us to derive results regarding how multi-agent systems can be applied to improve the effectiveness and survivability of end-to-end network services in dynamic, hostile environments.

Section 2 of the paper summarises the military application domain and proposes how agent technology can be exploited to useful effect. Section 3 defines autonomic behaviour and summarises our autonomic network control system architecture. Section 4 is an overview of the experimentation environment, including the case study that we are implementing. Section 5 provides conclusions and further work.

2   Applying Agents to Agile Mission Groups

A mission can be separated into a planning and preparation phase and an execution phase. The commander will be assigned the mission and prepare a plan to meet the mission objectives, given the resources he has been assigned and the time available until the mission will commence [1]. The forces and materiel made available are briefed, or configured, for a role in the mission according to the commander's intent. The resulting plan and formation may be refined repeatedly before deployment.

During the execution phase, the formed agile mission group sets out to achieve the objectives specified by the commander's intent according to, but not necessarily bound by, the agreed plan. The communication system structure should be congruent with the command structure, which is expressed by the TASKORG. The mission is complete once the mission objectives have been (or cannot be) satisfied.

In terms of the communication network, the commander can be assumed to have expert support from a signals officer and be able to call upon a number of skilled signallers to support his statement of intent and contribute to its satisfaction. Given this, the following sections describe current techniques for managing military radio networks and suggest how agent capabilities can be exploited to improve on them.

2.1   Review of Existing Practice

The need for every networked radio device to be configured arises from features of modern radio communication platforms (e.g. Bowman, SINCGARS) such as secure-voice, frequency-hopping, routing and delivery of data packets, support for multiple roles, authentication, and encryption. The previous generation (e.g. Clansman) were limited to unsecured broadcast speech using interfaces defined in hardware.

The current network management approach is a manually intensive off-line process that requires expert input from a planning cell throughout. While this is tolerable during planning and preparation, though cumbersome, it is ill-suited to execution where rapid replanning and dissemination may be required to respond to unforeseen events or transient conditions while maintaining pursuit of the mission objectives.

The current process can be summarised by considering that there is a management terminal on a network running a planning application. This terminal enables the operator to input the location and properties of each of the network devices, the network resources available to those devices, and the intended use of each of those devices and resources. The terminal will perform an analysis of the input and create a number of potential network configurations from which the operator can select the most appropriate, according to his expertise and judgement. Part of an individual device's configuration (a number of alternate fills) can be applied directly over the network. The management terminal also prepares fills that can be written to portable fill guns (data sticks) for manual application of device configuration information.

This presents a potential single point of failure, so the planning application can partition the problem hierarchically. This allows the planning and configuration activities to be distributed across the network and it permits configuration of a sub-network to be devolved to applications on a terminal local to that sub-network.

However, this requires an appropriately skilled operator at each local terminal who will communicate and collaborate with a number of peer and subordinate operators, and perhaps a supervisory operator. The performance (e.g. responsiveness, accuracy or robustness) of the network management system is reliant on the ability of operators to agree on a plan, to schedule the roll-out of update configurations, and to apply a new local configuration in precise conformance with that agreement.

Even in this case, errors and delays may propagate. If the model in the planning application (or its input) has a flaw, or conditions change to invalidate assumptions or predictions, then the plan may be invalid on application, leading to a need for a reconfiguration during execution. A new configuration must be created off-line (while the problem continues to affect the network) based on revised assumptions and predictions of network behaviour over some subset of the network devices, which may themselves be erroneous or invalidated by events when the new configuration is finally applied.

The management applications are separated from the targets of control, so there is a risk that a flaw or event that inhibits automatic dissemination of configuration information updates to a subset of the network devices can prevent a consistent, complete reconfiguration. This may create fragments that are out of automatic control, carrying an outdated configuration that can only be updated manually.

2.2 Exploiting Agent Capabilities

The management of a network in a dynamic and hostile environment presents a number of problems to which there is no static or single point solution. No control system can accurately and instantly discover the global state of a network, deduce the ideal global state, and implement a change to the ideal state.

Agents are not a magic bullet for this problem. However, they can provide a more appropriate mapping between the control system and the system being controlled, and automate many of the resulting control mechanisms. They can also accept delegation of those decision-making and collaboration functions that are more suited to machines than people, easing the burden on operators and providing a management system that can operate in an autonomic manner given appropriate high-level direction.

Specifically, there is potential to create a synergistic relationship between the operator and the agent system that manages the network, such that the operator is able to concentrate on high-level decision-making regarding the objectives that the network should satisfy, while the agent system is able to support and implement decisions more quickly, accurately and robustly under stress [6, 10, 13].

The operator can devolve those planning and configuration responsibilities, for which he has no need to remain in the loop, to the network devices themselves. A community of agents on a device can ensure that the device behaves appropriately within its peer group and provides suitable information to inform management decisions and monitor changes and events. A community of agents distributed amongst a peer group of devices can ensure that the group collaborates to achieve the objectives set for it by a superior (another agent or agent community, or an operator).

Hence, the planning and configuration application is the network. No additional off-line process is required to gather, deliver, model, decide and disseminate network configurations over the network. The operator will still require a specialised terminal application in order to interact with the management system, however this application could be located at any suitable network device in any suitable location and it will provide on-line access to the agent system, part of which is running continually throughout the network whether supervised or unsupervised.

In a similar way to that in which a surgeon can diagnose a medical condition from the symptoms of a patient, run tests to confirm the diagnosis and then treat, or perform surgery on, the living person, the agent system should enable the operator to diagnose network problems from symptoms and correct them to keep the network (and any separated parts) as viable and as capable as possible for as long as possible.

Assumptions and predictions provided by operators and agents regarding network behaviour may not be perfectly reliable and the models held by the agents may have flaws, as might the inputs from the system. However, given that there are no fundamental design flaws in the system as a whole, it is possible to design-in checks and balances to prevent a rogue agent, or operator, from imperilling the whole system.

Since the agents on the network devices are close to the targets of control, issued corrections can be executed automatically and directly with no mandatory off-line replanning process required. Fragmentation problems are eased since the smallest network fragment can control its own operation and reconfigure appropriately. It may not receive any further high-level direction, however the operator can rely on the fragment to maintain itself according to its original goals and the latest directions that reached it. Potential problems can be anticipated and managed until they are resolved on reintegration when the fragment will be able to report and collect new directions.

The use of agents is a cost in terms of the processing and storage overheads on network devices and the communication overheads between them. This is important since devices and networks in the military domain are designed for portability, robustness and resilience rather than computing power, raw throughput or efficiency.

In military radio networks, bandwidth is the most limited and limiting resource: it must be conserved at all times, used effectively, and preserved for critical messages. Also, its availability can vary dynamically and spatially in an unpredictable manner. A distributed multi-agent system approach to controlling the network must not add undue overhead or disrupt the progress of essential traffic through the network.

There is likely to be a compromise necessary between the intent and the resources made available to meet it. Military communications demands are intrinsically bursty, so there is a risk of intermittent transient events causing demand to exceed capacity.

Hence, the commander must articulate his priorities for the provision of information and communications services in support of the main effort expressed by his intent.

3 System Architecture

This section provides an overview of autonomic behaviour from the perspective of a military network and a high-level summary of our architecture for a network control system that can exhibit a range of autonomic behaviours. The architecture defines the services that are required to plan, configure and maintain a network in an autonomic manner, given direction from one, or more, levels of a command hierarchy.

3.1 Autonomic Behaviour

The commander's intent and priorities direct and inform control plane decisions through translation into policies that can be applied to influence control system behaviour and provide decision criteria where lower-level objectives conflict. [11]

The benefits of an autonomic control system should emerge where it can make unsupervised choices of actions in response to stimuli from the users and from the environment such that it maintains the viability of the network on which it is resident and, more importantly, supports the successful achievement of the objectives expressed by the commander's intent for the duration of a military operation.

We adapted the IBM autonomic manifesto [9] to apply to military contexts by addressing the hostility of the environment and ensuring that human decision-making predominates. Two important points are:

- The autonomic network must be directed by, and always act in support of, the commander's intent.
- It should be able to override its own sense of self-preservation, or the preservation of its parts, in order to achieve the objectives assigned to it.

For the purpose of implementing autonomic behaviours [10] within a network that acts as a telecommunications system in support of a military operation, we can summarise the essential responsibilities of the control plane of the system as:

- Interpret the commander's intent and provision of physical resources
- Provide appropriate feedback and reporting
- Satisfy the commander's intent by distributing and maintaining a virtual communication system over the physical network that provides the autonomic behaviours identified in Fig. 1.

Fig. 1 shows that self-configuration is the fundamental behaviour on which all of the others rely. The act of protecting against an event, or healing after it has occurred, will involve a reconfiguration of the live system, while self-optimisation will rely on reconfiguration should it require changes to the system state. Self-configuration is the mechanism by which the network is brought into existence. Amongst its first tasks, the network must adopt a viable configuration in order to fulfil its purpose within its environment. It must also be able to adapt into a new viable configuration, i.e. reconfigure, should its state, its purpose, or its environment change.

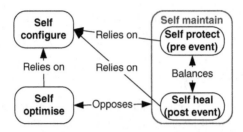

Fig. 1. Autonomic behaviours

The balance expressed by self-maintenance can be expressed as the extent to which the system plans ahead to ensure its survival or simply reacts once an event has occurred. For a military radio network, adverse events include variations in channel availability (or capacity), loss of line-of-sight, and the destruction of equipment.

The response to an event may depend on the current state of the system, its mission objectives and the environment. For example, if the delivery of a transmission is more important than the network remaining operational, then the control system may restrict its own management traffic and allocate all of its resources to that delivery. Alternatively, if network survival is more important, then it may drop user traffic.

Self-protection implies that the system will consider possible adverse events and plan to mitigate, or take advantage, of their effects in order to preserve its integrity and/or mission. Thus, the system may be able to avoid the occurrence, or mitigate the consequences, of an adverse event such that it does not endanger the viability of the system, or its achievement of its objectives.

Self-healing implies that the system will reconfigure to restore its integrity and/or purpose to complete its mission once an event has taken place. Healing may be the execution of a pre-planned response or an on-the-fly response based on the system's knowledge about itself, its environment and its purpose within that environment.

Unforeseeable events can be handled only by self-healing, however there will be a continual trade-off regarding foreseeable events. It can be argued that protection will consume greater resources while healing carries greater risk for a known event. It is possible for a single event to be addressed by both behaviours and for protective or healing action to lead to a further unforeseen adverse event.

There is also a trade-off between robustness (through self-maintenance) and optimisation. We prefer robustness (and similarly prefer effectiveness over efficiency) due to the complex, unpredictable, and hostile nature of the military environment.

3.2   Key Components of the Network Control System Architecture

The network control system can be expressed in terms of network devices, each of which contains a collection of agents and software objects providing the services shown in Fig. 2. Four types of service are identified: a control service, a policy service, a user service and a factory service (not shown). A factory service resides locally on a device and can create, destroy, and maintain instances of other services.

A control service monitors and controls the operation of any service that is not a policy service. A policy service encodes domain knowledge through which it can mediate the actions of any service. It may supply policy, or a policy decision, on request, or it may act independently of any request. The target service must enforce the policy supplied, unless it conflicts with an existing policy of greater importance.

A user service is a network resident service that responds to policy and control and provides characteristics that can be monitored. It may advertise itself to other services and other services may request that it provide them with its service. A user service specifies a generic service that may be customised to provide, or to support, any service that is directly, or indirectly, required by users of the network.

We can consider that the policy service is responsible for determining what state the user service should be directed towards. The control service is responsible for how the state of the user service is changed and maintained to achieve that state.

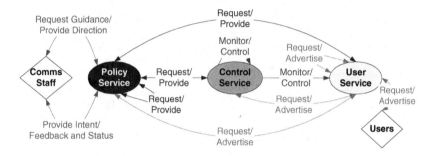

Fig. 2. Control of services mediated by policy

A user, control, or policy service may be a device-local service (local refers to encapsulation within the device) or it may participate in a virtual service that resides across a group of devices: such a service belongs to the group and not necessarily to any particular member. Virtual services are always remote (not wholly contained within the device) to other services, even to those resident on the same device.

The architecture for the network control system can be expressed as the interaction between a number of local and virtual services as shown in Fig. 3. Device-local services maintain a virtual device (resident on a physical device) that is responsible for creating and maintaining pipes, each of which represents an end-to-end connection to another virtual device over the underlying physical network. Virtual devices provide peer-to-peer communication with each other under the control of device-local services and regulate communication between users, applications and services.

Virtual services exist distributed across this network by some composition of local services over groups of virtual devices. Virtual services provide high-level policy and control services to the network control system and provide services that support interfaces between that system, the communication system (through the device-local services) and the administrators and users of the communication system.

Device-local services have an interface that allows access to host-local services (those services provided by other software resident on the device), some of which may be services that allow access to the platform to which the device is attached. Low-level local services provided by the virtual device will allow limited access to the physical device's characteristics and the physical network in which it participates.

Administrative services allow an administrative user to express intent (high level objectives) for the network, to receive status reports on the viability of the network

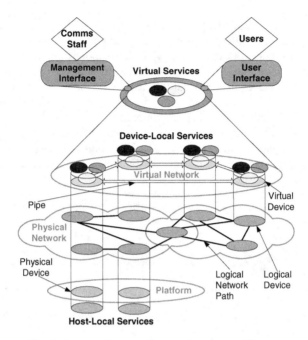

Fig. 3. Autonomic network control system architecture

and its ability to satisfy its intent, and to receive and respond to requests for guidance from the network. One important function of an administrative service that may be provided by agents is the conversion of a user's intent into policy input for high-level policy services (though this is currently outside the scope of this project).

4 Experimentation Environment

This section discusses the emulated network testbed on which experiments are conducted, the selection of toolkits for modelling and implementing agent systems and the design and implementation of the case study for concept demonstration.

4.1 Emulated Network Testbed

We have created an emulated network testbed to experiment with implementations of the architecture. A single machine can emulate a small network (five to ten linked devices on a desktop PC) using virtual images without using its physical network interface. A network of several hundred devices can be emulated by connecting host machines over a test network, which emulates the radio links that connect identified groups of virtual images (emulating vehicle intra-networks or man-pack radios) distributed amongst the hosts as determined by an experiment controller (Fig. 4).

Each host machine provides several vimages (virtual machine images), virtual network interfaces (that may be allocated to vimages), and emulated virtual network links. These coexist, isolated from the host or other instances, sharing the resources of the host (processing, memory, storage and networking). [14]

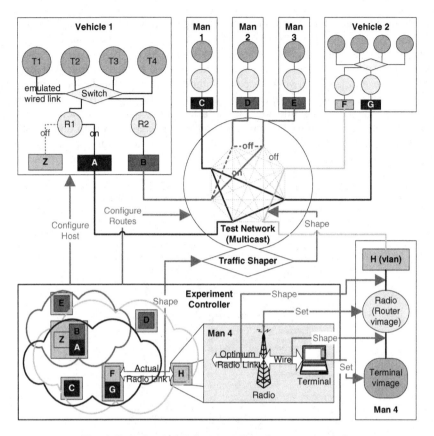

Fig. 4. Experimental radio network environment emulation

The virtual machine images emulate network devices, running any software that we require including user processes that communicate using the emulated network, network services and a multi-agent control system. Emulated network links within and between hosts rely on the test network to provide the end-to-end characteristics of the radio and wired links between network devices in a typical military deployment.

The experiment controller holds a representation of the network environment. This is applied to the entities and the connections between them by configuring the entities and the test network over a separate control network. It determines parameter settings, enabling or disabling of routes, and the shaping of links on enabled routes. Processes running isolated within vimages are accessible from the control network via bridges to protected virtual interfaces allowing user interaction, or external control.

The emulation is limited by the number of available hosts, and ultimately, by the capacity of the test network for providing the emulated radio links that share it. Experimentation on a larger scale is being investigated using network simulation [2].

4.2 Multi-agent System Implementation

The services described by the architecture will be implemented using the Cougaar agent toolkit to control software objects and to interact with a GUI. Cougaar is a Java-based framework developed under the DARPA sponsored Advanced Logistics (ALP) and Ultralog programs [8] for large-scale distributed agent-based applications.

The implementations of network control system services (Fig. 5) will be used for experiments and tests [5] using the emulated network testbed, which will provide them with an emulated network to control through the virtual device, which also enables the construction of multiple virtual networks using peer-to-peer mechanisms.

The implementation is informed by a reference model of system behaviour according to the architecture. For animation and experimentation with this model, we are using AnyLogic [3], a Java-based, extensible modelling framework combining continuous and discrete-event simulation with an agent-based modelling approach.

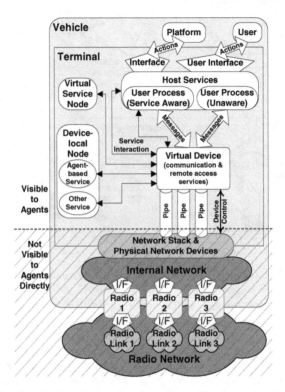

Fig. 5. Implementation of agent-based services within an emulated terminal

4.3 Agile Military Network Case Study

We envisage that one application for this technology is to provide an agile military network that can support the mission of its agile group of roaming users (Fig. 6).

The concept demonstration shows that an agent-based network control system can provide a viable autonomic network that exhibits simple autonomic behaviours. The autonomic network will demonstrate its ability to cope with the injection of some adverse events without any manual intervention and by its ability to provide feedback on the network environment so that the user can be informed of delays or outages and the administrator is provided with diagnostic reports, requests for guidance and decision support in dealing with severe disruption.

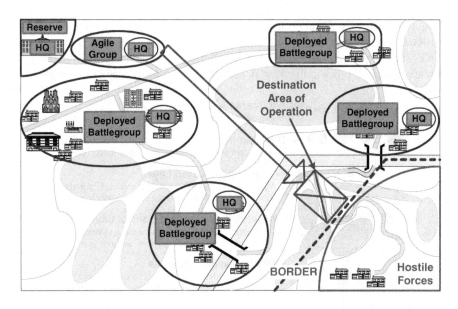

Fig. 6. A commander decides to occupy and control access to an area containing a border crossing. An agile task group (formed from the rear battlegroups and reserve) is assigned a mission to reconnoitre and then secure the area of operation, maintaining contact en route.

A basic agent-based network control system has been developed to deliver effective virtual network pipes and communities of interest that support the provision and maintenance of services for communicating peers as the agile mission group crosses boundaries between existing deployments. This may necessitate access to services on, and transit across, their networks and handover (and/or redundant provision) of services between them. The agile network is also able to avoid interference from (and with) existing networks or radio transmitters.

As it crosses between boundaries between zones, or enters the range of a new radio network operated by another group or transmitter, a peer in the agile group may:

- Avoid contact and/or interference (block access and monitor if potentially hostile).
- Find a matching radio configuration and negotiate access to it and its services.

Each zone provides a number of shared service communities to which access is regulated by the identity of the service or device requesting access and the identities of the user roles that it is representing. Each identity may belong to one or more groups with listen, talk and/or modify privileges for different services. These shared service communities are the equivalent of all-informed radio nets in current military network configurations. For example, they may relate to command, logistics, fire-control and so on, but have the advantage of flexible assignment as virtual networks. On discovery of an accessible friendly network in a zone, the agile group peer can:

- Discover services that service access points in the local zone will provide to it.
- Request a service that the network in the local zone will provide to it.
- Establish a point-to-point connection to a peer within the local zone.

- Request transit to, or local presentation of, a service from peer in a remote zone.
- Listen on one or more of the shared service communities in the local zone.
- Talk on one or more of the shared service communities in the local zone.
- Create or modify pipes in the overlay network to alter local zone virtual networks.

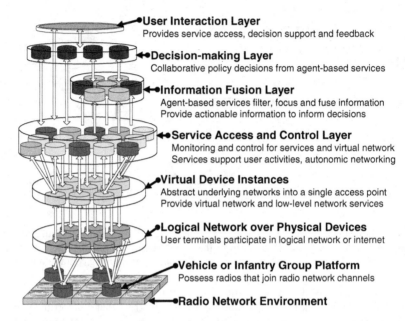

Fig. 7. A layered view of the case study implementation framework

The use of agent-based services within the case study can be summarised by Fig. 7. Users do not care whether services are provided by agents, but agents may be able to use such information to compose communities and societies across boundaries that provide higher-level services to, and on behalf of, users. Thus, there is a scale of interaction states between radio networks which can be controlled.

- network unaware (cannot detect other network(s))
- network aware (can detect other networks(s) but not interact at any level)
- network cooperative (share sufficient network characteristics to inter-network)
  - service unaware (cannot locate a Service Access Point on other network)
  - service aware (SAP located, but no service acquired, or access denied)
  - service cooperative (can negotiate access to services advertised by SAP)
    - agent unaware (don't know or don't care if the service is agent-based)
    - agent aware (may attempt negotiation, but language or permit not yet agreed)
    - agent cooperative (can form a community/society with the other agents)

We abstract the underlying radio networks behind the concept of a virtual device that resides on each physical device. It encapsulates and abstracts all of the network access mechanisms and low-level network communication services that the physical device can make available. Thus, an agent can be informed of interaction states up to service aware, but it cannot directly influence the transitions between those states other than through the mechanisms provided to it by the virtual device. Transitions above service aware are considered to be under the direct control of the agent system.

5 Conclusions and Future Work

Within the military environment, there is scope for the introduction of agent technology to help reduce the demands on signals staff as new and more complex network technology is introduced. One area in which agent systems can provide a practical advantage is in providing the flexible control system needed to allow an agile mission group to reconfigure their network through high level direction of an autonomic network, while maintaining a high tempo during mission execution.

We have proposed a service-based architecture for an autonomic network control system, in which agents provide policy and control services that ensure that a network will meet its objectives, given high-level direction from signals staff regarding its configuration and use of resources.

In the next project phase, we will develop incremental network control system software releases implementing the architecture in full. We will use the Cougaar framework to provide agent-based services that enable more complex autonomic behaviours with reference to our system models and our implementation will be evaluated using the experimentation environment. A more detailed implementation, of an extended version of the case study, is being developed to provide a platform for experimentation with different network control system strategies.

One advanced feature is associated with the formation of a multi-agent system from heterogeneous agents residing on heterogeneous networks in a coalition force. An example may involve the provision of transit and location services to partners.

The emulated test bed design provides the experiment controller with an interface that allows it to be driven by an interactive simulation provided by a synthetic environment representation of a military scenario (being developed by a separate project). This is being developed to support the extended case study implementation.

Experiments will compare the autonomic network control system implementation against a control case to show that autonomic control provides a measurable benefit for current and future agile military networks in terms of its ability to synthesise and maintain new network configurations, its ability to survive hostile conditions or attacks and its capability to discover and interoperate with (or avoid) other networks.

We envisage that autonomic control can significantly improve the effectiveness, robustness and reliability of essential communication services for agile mobile forces and enable more flexible and rapid deployment of such forces.

Our aim is to develop an implementation that is mature enough (in the experimentation environment) to be allowed to progress into field-testing with a real military radio network and real end-user terminals.

Acknowledgements

This work is supported by the UK MOD Data and Information Fusion Defence Technology Centre.

References

1. Network Enabled Capability, JSP 777 (Edition 1). Ministry of Defence, January 2005. http://www.mod.uk/linked_files/issues/nec/nec_jsp777.pdf
2. Barr R., Haas Z.J., and van Renesse R.: JiST: Embedding Simulation Time into a Virtual Machine. Proceedings of the 5th EuroSim Congress on Modelling and Simulation, 2004.
3. Borshchev A. and Filippov A.: From System Dynamics and Discrete Event to Practical Agent Based Modeling: Reasons, Techniques, Tools. The 22nd International Conference of the System Dynamics Society, 2004.
4. Boutaba R. and Xiao J.: Network Management: State of the Art. Proceedings of IFIP World Computer Congress (WCC'02) TC6 Stream on Communication Systems: The State of the Art, pp. 127-146, 2002.
5. Edmonds B. and Bryson J.J.: The Insufficiency of Formal Design Methods – the necessity of an experimental approach for the understanding and control of complex MAS. Proceedings of AAMAS-2004, pages 938-945, 2004.
6. Foster I., Jennings N.R., and Kesselman C.: Brain Meets Brawn: Why Grid and Agents Need Each Other. Proceedings of the 3rd International Joint Conference on Autonomous Agents and Multi-Agent Systems (AAMAS-2004), pages 8-15, 2004.
7. Helsinger A., Kleinmann K., and Brinn M. A.: Framework to Control Emergent Survivability of Multi-Agent Systems. Proceedings of AAMAS-2004, pages 28-35, 2004.
8. Helsinger A. and Wright T.: Cougaar: A Robust Configurable Multi-Agent Platform. Proceedings of IEEEAC2005, paper 1412 Version 2, 2004.
9. Horn P.: Autonomic computing: IBM's Perspective on the State of Information Technology. 2001. http://www.research.ibm.com/autonomic/manifesto/
10. Kephart J.O. and Chess D.M.: The vision of Autonomic Computing. IEEE Computer, January 2003.
11. Kephart J.O. and Walsh W.E.: An Artificial Intelligence Perspective on Autonomic Computing Policies. Fifth IEEE International Workshop on Policies for Distributed Systems and Networks, 3-12, 2004.
12. Parunak, H.V.D. and Brueckner, S.A.: Stigmergic Learning for Self-Organising Mobile Ad-hoc Networks (MANET's). Proceedings of AAMAS 2004, pages 1324-1331, 2004.
13. Tesauro G. et al.: A Multi-Agent Systems Approach to Autonomic Computing. Proceedings of AAMAS-2004, pages 464-471, 2004.
14. Zec M.: Implementing a Clonable Network Stack in the FreeBSD Kernel. Proceedings of the 2003 USENIX Annual Technical Conference, 2003.

Representing Dispositions and Emotions
in Simulated Combat

H. Van Dyke Parunak, Robert Bisson, Sven Brueckner,
Robert Matthews, and John Sauter

Altarum Institute, 3520 Green Court, Suite 300
Ann Arbor, MI 48105-1579 USA
{van.parunak, robert.bisson, sven.brueckner,
robert.matthews, john.sauter}@altarum.org

Abstract. Emotion is an essential element of human behavior. Particularly in stressful situations such as combat, it is at least as important as rational analysis in determining a participant's behavior. Yet combat models routinely ignore this factor. DETT (Disposition, Emotion, Trigger, Tendency) is an environmentally mediated model of emotion that captures the essential features of the widely-used OCC (Ortony, Clore, Collins) model in a computationally tractable framework that can support large numbers of combatants. We motivate and describe this architecture, and report preliminary experiments that use it in simulating combat scenarios.

1 Introduction

Simulation and modeling are extensions of the experimental method for studying systems. Direct experimentation is the approach of choice when the systems in question are common (so that one can find instances for study), malleable (open to manipulation by the experimenter, so that one can fix some variables while varying others), and observable (so that one can see the results of experimental manipulations). When these conditions are not met in the real world, a computer model can provide them in a simulated one.

Real-world warfare lacks malleability and observability. Making deliberate changes in the face of combat is extremely difficult, a phenomenon that the Prussian General Carl von Clausewitz termed the "friction of war," and their outcome is obscure not only to those participating in the conflict, but sometimes also to historians years after, a situation he called "fog" [20]. Thus it is not surprising that the military is one of the leading users of simulation and modeling, in understanding how combat situations develop and how commanders and troops should respond. In spite of their approximate character, simulations can greatly increase the users' insight into the real system.

Emotion is an essential element of human behavior. Particularly in stressful situations such as combat, it is at least as important as rational analysis in determining a participant's behavior. Yet combat models routinely ignore this factor. DETT (Disposition, Emotion, Trigger, Tendency) is an environmentally mediated model of emotion that captures the essential features of the widely-used OCC (Ortony, Clore,

S.G. Thompson and R. Ghanea-Hercock (Eds.): DAMAS 2005, LNAI 3890, pp. 51–65, 2006.

Collins [13]) model in a computationally tractable framework. A unique feature of our approach is the definition of a Disposition parameter to distinguish different agents' susceptibility to various emotions.

In Section 3, we review previous work in both combat modeling and computational emotions. Section 4 describes the DETT model. Section 5 reports on some experiments with the model. Section 6 concludes.

2 Previous Work

Our work is related to two bodies of previous work: a long tradition of computer-assisted combat modeling, and more recent research on computational models of emotion.

2.1 Combat Modeling

The roots of combat modeling go back well before the computer era, and follow two distinct lines, one mathematical and the other behavioral.

2.1.1 Mathematical Models

Mathematical models of combat are of two types: Lanchester theory and game theory.

Lanchester Theory. In 1916, F.W. Lanchester published a set of differential equations that expressed how the change in strength of each side in a conflict varies with the current strength of the other side [9]. In their simplest form, his equations define the evolution through time of the strength of the two sides, $R(t)$ and $B(t)$, as a function of the effective firing rates α_R and α_B of the two sides, $\dfrac{dR}{dt} = -\alpha_B B(t)$; $\dfrac{dB}{dt} = -\alpha_R R(t)$.

His system is formally equivalent to the Lotka-Voltera equations for predator-prey populations. An early application of computers to military modeling was integrating the Lanchester equations, and many of the military's leading models today are still based on refinements of this model, for example, the Bonder-Farrell Attrition Algorithm equations [1].

Game Theory. Game theory was originally developed in context of economic analysis [21, 22], but after WWII, it became a central tool for military planning at the DoD-sponsored RAND Institute and elsewhere. Game theory focuses on the rationality of the parties in conflict, and assumes that each seeks to maximize its own utility while recognizing that the other party is seeking to do the same.

Game theory and Lanchester theory differ in two important ways.

1. Lanchester theory models combatants as physical forces with no rationality. Game theory assumes that players are rational and seek to maximize a utility function.
2. Lanchester theory describes the evolution of combat through time. Game theory in its simplest form is concerned with the final outcome.

In spite of these differences, the two mathematical theories are similar in two ways.

1. They treat the opposing sides as aggregates, and do not consider the detailed interactions of the individual soldiers and weapons of which they are composed.

2. They lump the effect of emotions with other factors (e.g., firepower or positional advantage) and thus do not permit them to be studied in their own right.

2.1.2 Behavioral Models

Behavioral models are exemplified by wargames, either with real troops or on sand tables on which experimenters alternatively move playing pieces to explore tactics. Inexpensive computers and multi-agent techniques permit models of combat in which each entity is represented by an individual computer agent.

Such models are superior to traditional mathematical models because they can capture the individual evolution of interacting entities, rather than modeling them as averages over the population. Combat interactions are strongly nonlinear, and population averages often miss important divergences in individual trajectories. As a result, entity-based models can often yield more realistic results than do Lanchester or game-theoretic models.

A disadvantage of agent-based models is that they can require more computation than classical mathematical models. Fortunately, relatively simple entity models, embedded in an environment based on cellular automata, are often sufficient to capture much of the complexity of warfare [6]. One explanation for this outcome is the phenomenon of universality [16], which recognizes that the structure of interactions may overwhelm differences in the processing carried out by individual agents.

Once a model represents individual soldiers, it can address emotional characteristics.

Thus, for instance, EINSTein [6] represents an agent's personality as a set of six weights, each in [-1, 1], describing the agent's response to six kinds of information. Four of these describe the number of alive friendly, alive enemy, injured friendly, and injured enemy troops within the agent's sensor range. The other two weights relate to the model's use of a childhood game, "capture the flag," as a prototype of combat. Each team has a flag, and seeks to protect it from the other team while simultaneously capturing the other team's flag. The fifth and sixth weights describe how far the agent is from its own and its adversary's flag. A positive weight indicates that the agent is attracted to the entity described by the weight, while a negative weight indicates that it is repelled.

MANA [10] extends the concepts in EINSTein. Friendly and enemy flags are replaced by the waypoints being pursued by each side. MANA includes four additional components: low, medium, and high threat enemies. In addition, it defines a set of triggers (e.g., reaching a waypoint, being shot at, making contact with the enemy, being injured) that shift the agent from one personality vector to another. A default state defines the personality vector when no trigger state is active.

The notion of being attracted or repelled by friendly or adversarial forces in various states of health is an important component of what we informally think of as emotion (e.g., fear, compassion, aggression), and the use of the term "personality" in both EINSTein and MANA suggests that the system designers are thinking anthropomorphically, though they do not use "emotion" to describe the effect they are trying to achieve.

2.2 Emotional Modeling

The study of emotion has a rich history in the psychological and physiological literature, reaching back well over a century [4], and has produced a wide range of theories, identifying emotions with outward expressions, physiological responses, distinct behaviors, or cognitive processes, among others.

Agent-based software is growing in two areas where realistic simulation of human behavior is important: agent-based modeling, and human interfaces (including gaming). This growth has led to a flurry of interest in computational models of emotion [18], each drawing on different segments of the psychological tradition.

Emotion clearly has facets related to an organism's outward expressions and physiological reactions, important for applications in human interfaces and robotics (e.g., [11, 12]). For our purposes, a cognitive perspective on emotions is more appropriate, and we draw on the OCC model [13]. The fundamental insight of this model is that emotions are "valenced reactions to events, agents or objects, with their particular nature being determined by the way in which the eliciting situation is construed." That is, the strength of a given emotion depends on the events, agents, or objects in the environment of the agent exhibiting the emotion. Their presence is mapped to a "valence," a positive or negative score, by a process called "assessment" or "appraisal."

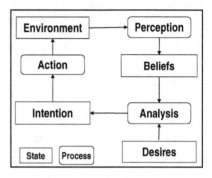

Fig. 1. BDI Data Flow

Once an emotion exists, it impacts the subject in several ways. It focuses attention, increases the pro- minence of an event in memory, affects cognitive style and performance, and influences judgments [2]. In particular, according to OCC, "behavior is a res- ponse to an emotional state in conjunct-tion with a particular initiating event."

In our application, we focus on the impact of emotion on an agent's analysis and judgment, the process by which it selects its intentions from its desires.

To put this system in a broader perspective, consider the basic Belief-Desire-Intention [17, 19] data flow summarized in Fig. 1. Beliefs (derived

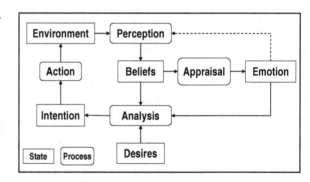

Fig. 2. BDI enhanced with OCC

from the environment by perception) and Desires (which are constant over the time horizon of our model) feed an analysis process that produces Intentions, which in turn drive actions that change the environment.

Fig. 2 shows a simple enhancement of this model with the OCC model of emotion. Beliefs feed not only analysis, but also the appraisal process that generates emotions. These emotions in turn influence analysis and perception (the latter link shown dashed because we do not emphasize it in our current system).

Gratch and Marsella [5] offer one of the more mature current computational models of agent emotion. Fig. 3 sketches their model, and Table 1 summarizes the correspondence between salient elements of Fig. 2 and Fig. 3.

The decision systems in EINSTein and MANA are subsets of Fig. 2.

Fig. 3. Gratch-Marsella Model of Cognitive-Motivational-Emotive System ([5], Fig. 2)

Fig. 4 casts EINSTein in this framework. EINSTein's personality vector guides the agent's decisions, but is itself fixed, and does not change in response to the agent's beliefs about the events, objects, or agents in its environment. Thus it is not a "valenced reaction," but a representation of the agent's desires. In this sense, EINSTein does not capture emotion.

Fig. 5 shows MANA. Because MANA's personality vectors depend on a trigger state, they qualify as a valenced reaction. The default personality vector that applies when no trigger state is active continues to represent the agent's desires.

Table 1. Comparison of Models

BDI + OCC (Fig. 2)	Gratch-Marsella (Fig. 3)
Environment	Environment
Perception	Causal Interpretation
Beliefs	Causal Interpretation
Appraisal	Appraisal
Emotion	Affective State
Analysis	Coping
Desires	???
Intention	Control Signals
Action	Action

In both EINSTein and MANA, analysis consists of multiplying the environmental information available to the agent by the personality vector, directly yielding a movement vector to guide the agent's subsequent actions. In both models, the perception process is represented by a vision radius within which the agent has perfect knowledge of its environment. These processes are considerably simpler than the mechanisms of symbolic AI applied in [5]

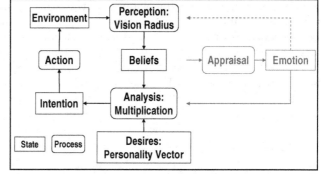

Fig. 4. EINSTein as BDI + OCC

for the same func-
tions. The differ-
ences reflect the
differing objectives of
the systems. Gratch
and Marsella are
supporting a training
environment with
relatively few agents,
and regular inter-
action with humans
slows the pace to the
point that significant
computation can occ-

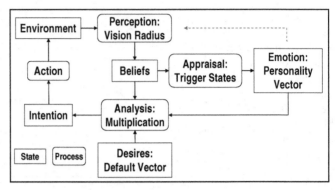

Fig. 5. MANA as BDI + OCC

ur. EINSTein and MANA manipulate dozens or even hundreds of agents in
simulations of combat without human interaction, and need to minimize the overall
execution time to permit the execution of many instances of a scenario.

3   The DETT Emotion Model

Our work is supported by two DoD projects that require the ability to simulate large
numbers of combatants very rapidly. Thus we favor numerical computation.

3.1   Application Contexts

DETT was developed in the context of the DARPA RAID program, and is also being
used to model noncombatants in another project.

The objective of RAID [8] is to anticipate enemy actions and deceptions, in order
to provide real-time support to a tactical commander. We are constructing a module
that reasons about the adversary's likely state and actions (thus, an Adversarial Reasoning Module, or ARM). Our particular ARM synergizes three distinct tactical rea-
soners: statistical reasoning for early detection of anomalous situations that might
indicate risk[1], knowledge-based inference to reason about possible agent goals[2], and
behavioral evolution and extrapolation, using swarms of fine-grained agents to explore possible futures of the battlespace [15]. In this third reasoner, we evolve
agents against observed reality to learn their characteristics and determine which
ones are most likely to reflect future behavior. Because many of these agents must
execute faster than real time, they cannot conduct complex symbolic reasoning, but
use numerical computation. These agents use the DETT model.

In the other project, MAROP (Multi-Agent Representation of the Operational Environment), we are developing methods to enrich a new military modeling system
(Combat XXI) by automating the reactions of non-combatants with combatants. This

---

[1] This process, known as SAD (Statistical Anomaly Detection), is developed by our colleagues
    Rafael Alonso, Hua Li, and John Asmuth at Sarnoff Corporation.
[2] This process, known as KIP (Knowledge-based Intention Projection), is developed by our
    colleagues Paul Nielsen, Jacob Crossman, and Rich Frederiksen at Soar Technology.

capability requires us to recognize that non-combatants will have a range of personality types and to incorporate these differences in their behavior.

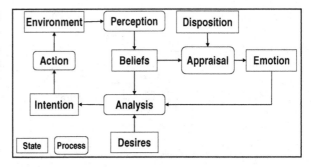

Fig. 6. Incorpcorating Disposition in BDI + OCC

3.2 Architecture

We need a computationally efficient way to take emotional tendencies into account in modeling combat. This reasoning takes place at two locations in Fig. 2: Appraisal and Analysis. We have defined numerical methods for both of these.

3.2.1 Appraisal

MANA's use of triggered personality vectors that specify numerical weights for translating beliefs into intentions is a useful model for appraisal, but has two limitations. First, MANA defines vectors and triggers at the level of the squad, and all members of the squad share the same values. In practice, individual combatants will differ widely in their susceptibility to different emotions. A firefight that might stimulate high fear in a new soldier may have much less effect on a seasoned veteran. In order to use evolution to learn the characteristics of entities, we must parameterize this kind of difference. Second, MANA assumes that an agent in the presence of a trigger immediately adopts the associated emotion, and that when the trigger is removed, the emotion ceases immediately. Empirically, the rise of an emotion, while rapid, is not instantaneous, and the emotion will persist for a while after the trigger is removed.

To address the first concern we add a new component, Dispositions, to the model (Fig. 6). There is a one-to-one mapping between Emotions and Dispositions. Like Desires, Dispositions are persistent (that is, their values are constant over the time horizon of our simulations). A Disposition modulates Appraisal to determine the extent to which a given belief triggers the corresponding emotion. The emotion then modulates Analysis to impose a Tendency on the resulting intention. The main elements of this model are thus the Disposition, Emotion, Trigger (the beliefs that lead to the emotion), and Tendency (the effect on intentions) (DETT). Table 2 illustrates two Dispositions, with their associated Emotions and illustrative Triggers and Tendencies.

Table 2. Sample DETT Semantics

Disposition	Emotion	Trigger	Tendency
Cowardice	Fear	Presence of armed enemy Incoming attack	Less attention to orders Tend to move away from threat
Irritability	Anger	Presence of enemy	More likely to engage in combat Tend to move toward threat

Our agents live in a digital phero-mone infrastructure [3]. Agents sense one another's pres-ence through la-beled scalars that they deposit in the environment and that diffuse spa-tially and evaporate over time. The dy-namics of these pheromones models

Table 3. Pheromone Flavors in RAID

RedAlive	Emitted by a living or dead entity of the appropri-ate group (Red = enemy, Blue = friendly, Green = neutral)
RedCasualty	
BlueAlive	
BlueCasualty	
GreenAlive	
GreenCasualty	
WeaponsFire	Emitted by a firing weapon
KeySite	Emitted by a site of particular importance to Red
Cover	Emitted by locations that afford cover from fire
Mobility	Emitted by roads and other structures that en-hance agent mobility

(very crudely) the Perception process that maps environmental reality into agent be-liefs: an agent believes what it senses in the form of pheromones in its environment. Table 3 summarizes our pheromone vocabulary in the case of RAID.

Let P be the vector of pheromone strengths at an agent's location. The agent's Dispo-sition is a matrix D. $D[i,j] \in [0,1]$ is the relevance of the ith pheromone flavor to the jth emotion. The agent's jth emotion depends (nonlinearly) on the jth element of $P^T D$.

To allow emotions to vary realistically in time, agents have internal pheromones [17] (digital "hormones"), one for each Emotion. $P^T D$ at a given time step determines the deposit to the vector E of emotion hormones at that time step, so the longer an agent is exposed to a trigger pheromone, the higher the level of the associated emo-tion grows. When the relevant trigger is removed, the corresponding emotion decays exponentially. Also, the higher the disposition, the more quickly the associated emo-tion grows in the presence of a trigger. An agent with high irritability will grow angry faster in the presence of a triggering pheromone than an agent with low irritability.

3.2.2 Analysis

Analysis draws on the same pheromone vector P of beliefs as does Appraisal, and takes as input the current state of the emotion vector E. In addition, it considers the values of the agent's vector of Desires or Wants W. The desires we are modeling are Protect Red, Protect Blue, Protect Green, Protect Key Sites, Avoid Combat, Avoid Detection, and Survive. Each has a real value in the range [-1,1], where a negative value indicates that the agent wants the opposite state of affairs described by the de-sire. A movement matrix M indicates whether a given Desire tends to attract or repel the agent toward a given flavor of pheromone: $M[i,j]$ is 1 if desire j is attracted to pheromone i, -1 if it is repelled, and 0 if the pheromone is irrelevant to the desire.

In the absence of emotions, the agent's behavior is a function (again nonlinear) of $P^T M W$. Emotions modulate these behaviors. Elevated Anger will increase movement likelihood, weapon firing likelihood, and tendency toward an exposed posture, while elevated Fear will decrease these likelihoods. Level of a particular emotion actually models the extent to which the emotion modulates the agent's behavior. Someone who experiences high fear, but is able to continue to behave as if he were not afraid, would be modeled as having low fear. We are not trying to model emotion as experienced by an agent, only emotion that can be perceived by its impact on the agent's behavior.

4 Experimental Results

We report here the initial experiments that we are conducting in the context of the two projects that are using the DETT model.

4.1 MAROP

Our initial experiments measure the effect of the emotions of fear and anger on the spatial correlation of non-combatants with other entities of interest. All experiments are conducted on a road network modeling an urban area. In our experimental schema, Red and Blue forces follow scripted movements that carry them from opposite sides of the town to a central location where they engage in a firefight. Initially, Green agents are distributed randomly throughout the town.

MAROP uses a simplified version of DETT in which different dispositions and emotions are precompiled into an agent's attrac-

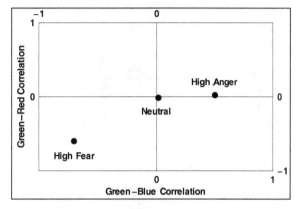

Fig. 7. Effect of Emotions in MAROP (notional data)

Table 4. Emotional Tendencies in MAROP

Pheromone	Fear	Anger
RedAlive	Repulsive	Neutral
BlueAlive	Repulsive	Attractive
GreenAlive	Attractive	Neutral
WeaponsFire	Repulsive	Attractive

tion to or repulsion from each of four different pheromone flavors: RedAlive, BlueAlive, GreenAlive, and WeaponsFire. We define two emotions, Fear and Anger, as summarized in Table 4. (These encodings assume that the combat takes place on Red's "turf."). We can measure the resulting effect on the relative distribution of Green and each of the other classes (Red agents, Blue agents, and conflict events) by computing the spatial correlation of the associated pheromone fields. A correlation of 1 indicates that the two classes of agents tend to be in the same regions of the town, while a correlation of -1 indicates that they tend to avoid one another.

Distinct scenarios are run with Green agents coded as fearful, angry, and unemotional. Thus each experimental scenario forms a point in a three-dimensional space. Fig. 7 shows a projection of this space on the plane defined by Green-Red and Green-Blue correlations, illustrating how Green agents of different emotional configuration assume different relations to the other agents in the scenario.

4.2 RAID

RAID [15] uses our polyagent technology [14]. Each real-world entity has one agent representative, its avatar, but the avatar explores alternative possible futures by constantly sending out a swarm of ghosts whose pheromone-based self-organization then guides the avatars. Each ghost interacts with phero-mones deposited by all other entities in the world, and its emotional state is driven by those in-teractions.

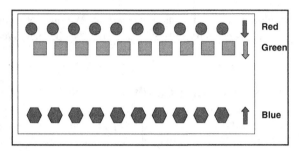

Fig. 8. Experimental Configuration for RAID

To test the effect of emotions in RAID, we arrange ten units (one avatar per unit) of each color in files, and have the Red and Green march through the Blue in formation (Fig. 8). When a file reaches one extreme of the arena, it reverses its direction. The units reach their original locations after 189 time steps, and the scenario repeats. Thus the units re-peatedly pass thro-ugh one another, depositing phero-

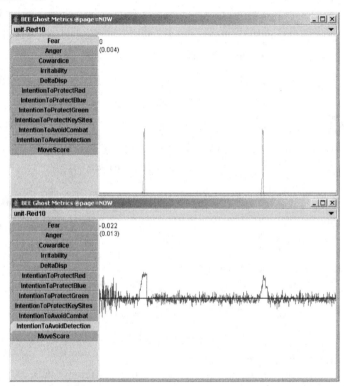

Fig. 9. Fear emotion (top) and intent to avoid detection (bottom) re-sulting from Cowardice disposition in the presence of adversarial pheromone. X-axis is time.

mones that indicate their presence and sensing the pheromones deposited by the other agents. Each unit emits eight ghosts per time step, and each ghost explores the future for five time steps before dying.

Each avatar's ghosts are generated with random values of "cowardice" in [0,1]. In our full system, an evolutionary process narrows these down on the basis of comparisons between the ghosts and actual history, but this process is not operating in this experiment. Averaged over time, each avatar's ghosts have a cowardice of 0.5.

The combination of a disposition with beliefs about the environment yields emotions (Fig. 6). Fig. 9 (top) shows the average value of the "fear" emotion across the ghosts for Red unit #1, as a function of time. This value peaks each time the unit crosses the line of Blue units, reflecting an interaction between the ghosts' cowardice disposition and the BlueAlive pheromone that they sense in the environment.

Emotion affects the agent's analysis to determine its intentions (Fig. 6). Fig. 9 (bottom) shows the average level of the "avoid detection" intention across this unit's ghosts. As required by Section 3, this intention increases when fear is active.

The net effect is thus to modulate the agent's intrinsic desire to avoid detection on the basis of its emotional state (specifically, fear), as determined by its disposition (cowardice) and its beliefs about the environment (the presence of adversaries).

We have subsequently tested the DETT model in a series of wargames involving human players who make decisions that are played out in a battlefield simulator. The commander for each side (Red and Blue) has at his disposal a team of pucksters, human operators who set waypoints for individual units in the simulator. Each unit corresponds to a fire team. Each puckster is responsible for four to six units. The simulator moves the units, determines firing actions, and resolves the outcome of conflicts.

Our system fits the DETT model to observed behavior of units, using evolution in a faster-than-real-time simulation of the battle [15]. To test our ability to fit personalities based on behavior, one Red puckster responsible for four units is designated the "emotional" puckster. He selects two of his units to be cowardly ("chickens") and two to be irritable ("Rambos"). He does not disclose this assignment during the run. He moves each unit according to the commander's orders until the unit encounters circumstances that would trigger the emotion associated with the unit's disposition. Then he manipulates chickens as though they are fearful (avoiding combat and moving away from Blue), and moves Rambos into combat as quickly as possible.

The difference between the two disposition values (Cowardice – Irritability) of the fittest ghosts proves a better indicator of the emotional state of the corresponding entity than either value by itself. To characterize a unit's personality, we maintain a 800-second exponentially weighted moving average of the Delta Disposition, and declare the unit to be a Chicken or Rambo if this value passes a negative or positive threshold, respectively. Currently, this threshold is set at 0.25. We are exploring additional filters. For example, a rapid rate of increase enhances the likelihood of calling a Rambo; units that seek to avoid detection and avoid combat are more readily called Chicken.

In one series of experiments, we successfully identified 68% of the chickens played. The detection rate for Rambos was much lower (5%), because the brave die young and our algorithm does not have enough exposure to a brave unit's behavior to diagnose its emotional state. But we never called a Rambo a Chicken. In the one case where we called a Chicken a Rambo, logs show that in fact the unit was being played aggressively, rushing toward oncoming Blue forces.

In addition to these results on units intentionally played as emotional, BEE sometimes detects other units as cowardly or brave. Analysis of the behavior of these units shows that these characterizations were appropriate: units that flee in the face of enemy forces or weapons fire are detected as Chickens, while those that stand their ground or rush the adversary are denominated as Rambos.

We did not detect some units that were played as cowardly. Many of these non-identified cowards were red units that were far from a blue unit. This discrepancy arises from an instructive difference between our software and the emotional puckster.

In our software, an agent's knowledge of its environment is conveyed entirely through the field of digital pheromones. If a red unit is beyond the propagation limit of the digital pheromone representing the blue unit, the red unit does not know of the existence of the blue unit. (The propagation limit on the pheromone is analogous to a limitation on a soldier's field of vision in the real world.) Thus even if the red unit has a cowardly disposition, it will not develop fear and will not behave in a fearful way.

The puckster looks down on a map of the overall battlespace, and can see all of the units at once. Confronted with managing several units concurrently in the midst of an active battle, the puckster can easily overlook the fact that though he can see both a red unit and a blue unit, the red unit might *not* be able to see the blue unit at a given moment. He knows that a fearful red should flee from blue. He can see both the red and the blue. So he moves the red away from the blue.

In DETT, emotions become active only when triggered. The inconsistency between what is played and what is detected is in what the cowardly agent believes about its environment. The puckster imputes his knowledge of blue to the red unit, so from his perspective its behavior reflects fear. In the software, the red agent does not see the blue unit, and so does not sense fear or act in a fearful manner. This example makes clear that emotion is very much a situated concept. It cannot be detected by movement away from a threat, only by movement away from a threat that the agent perceives. An emotion such as fear may well have triggers that we have not modeled, and our current approach would not detect it. The problem is circular in structure: we cannot recognize a behavior as evidence of fear unless we can associate it with a trigger, and we cannot learn that an environmental feature is a trigger unless we can detect that it causes fear. Breaking this closed loop is an interesting and challenging research question.[3]

5 Conclusion

A natural step in the development of combat models is the implementation of combatant emotion. The realities of human combat make this refinement necessary, while the maturation of agent-based models of combat makes it feasible. The Gratch-Marsella model offers a sophisticated implementation of current psychological theories of emotion, but is computationally too expensive to apply to large populations of combatant agents. Some fine-grained agent-based models embed a notion of personality (EINSTein and MANA), but do not recognize the important distinctions between individual combatants.

The DETT model (Dispositions, Emotions, Triggers, Tendencies) combines the theoretical richness of the Gratch-Marsella model with the computational efficiency of EINSTein and MANA. DETT was designed to reason about agents from the perspective of an external observer. Thus it is unabashedly a situated, behavioral model.

---

[3] We are grateful to a participant in the DAMAS workshop for a question that motivates this discussion.

- DETT is situated because it views emotion as arising in response to some environmental Trigger. If an element of an agent's internal state is generated autonomously by the agent independent of the agent's perception of the environment, DETT will not characterize it as an emotion. Interesting cases arise when an agent's perceptions are faulty. For example, an agent may perceive a threat where there is none, or may fail to perceive a real agent. Unless DETT has access to the agent's internal perceptions, it will not correctly characterize emotions in these cases.
- DETT is behavioral because it requires an emotion to manifest itself in some outward Tendency. It does not model internal feelings that have no outward effect. DETT does not distinguish an agent that feels fear but behaves as though it did not, and one that feels no fear. One might imagine an agent that reasons actively over its emotional state and overcomes its emotions through resolve. It is likely that such an agent would have slower response and other signs of tentativeness that might be detected externally. If the internal state has no impact on external behavior, though, DETT does not recognize it as an emotion.

For the applications for which DETT was developed, these limitations are appropriate. We are estimating emotional state from past observed responses to the environment, in order to predict future external behavior. Speculations about internal states that are not driven by the environment and that do not lead to an observable tendency are a distraction from this mission. In the contexts in which we have applied the model, it performs well.

DETT is still an approximation. It does not implement the known effect of emotion on perception, and does not consider other possible linkages (e.g., between emotion and desire). Such simplifications are in the nature of simulation, and are justified empirically by the notion of "universality": the dynamics of a multi-agent simulation often depend more on the interactions of the agents than on the details of individual agents' reasoning [16].

Ongoing research includes embedding this mechanism in an evolutionary loop that compares simulated behavior with real-world status to estimate the emotional state of observed combatants. This work shows how one agent can deduce the emotional state of other agents by observing their external behavior, and thus enables one to close the loop across agents through their shared environment. We are also developing methods for verifying and validating DETT against actual human behavior.

Acknowledgements

This material is based in part upon work supported by the Defense Advanced Research Projects Agency (DARPA) under Contract No. NBCHC040153. Any opinions, findings and conclusions or recommendations expressed in this material are those of the author(s) and do not necessarily reflect the views of the DARPA or the Department of Interior-National Business Center (DOI-NBC). Distribution Statement "A" (Approved for Public Release, Distribution Unlimited).

This study was supported in part by the TRADOC Analysis Center, Naval Post Graduate School, Monterey under Contract No. GS-35F-4912H, Order No. GST0904BH6603. The views and conclusions in this document are those of the authors and should not be interpreted as representing the official policies, either expressed or implied, of the TRADOC Analysis Center the Naval Post Graduate School, the Department of Defense, or the US Government.

References

[1] S. Bonder and L. W. Farrell. Development of Models for Defense Systems Planning. SRL 2147 TR70-2, Systems Research Laboratory, University of Michigan, Ann Arbor, MI, 1970.

[2] S. Brave and C. Nass. Emotion in Human-Computer Interaction. In J. A. Jacko and A. Sears, Editors, *The human-computer interaction handbook: fundamentals, evolving technologies and emerging applications*, pages 81-96. Lawrence Erlbaum Associates, Inc., Mahwah, NJ, 2003.

[3] S. Brueckner. *Return from the Ant: Synthetic Ecosystems for Manufacturing Control.* Dr.rer.nat. Thesis at Humboldt University Berlin, Department of Computer Science, 2000.   http://dochost.rz.hu-berlin.de/dissertationen/brueckner-sven-2000-06-21/PDF/Brueckner. pdf.

[4] C. Darwin. *The expression of the emotions in man and animals.* London, John Murray, 1872.

[5] J. Gratch and S. Marsella. A Domain-independent Framework for Modeling Emotion. *Journal of Cognitive Systems Research*, 5(4):269-306, 2004.

[6] A. Ilachinski. *Artificial War: Multiagent-based Simulation of Combat.* Singapore, World Scientific, 2004.

[7] D. Kinny, M. Georgeff, and A. Rao. A Methodology and Modelling Technique for Systems of BDI Agents. In W. VandeVelde and J. W. Perram, Editors, *Agents Breaking Away. 7th European Workshop on Modelling Autonomous Agents in a Multi-Agent World (MAAMAW'96). Lecture Notes in Artificial Intelligence 1038*, pages 56-71. Springer, Berlin, 1996. ftp://www.aaii.com.au/pub/aaii-technotes/technote58.ps.gz.

[8] A. Kott. Real-Time Adversarial Intelligence & Decision Making (RAID). 2004. http://dtsn.darpa.mil/ixo/programdetail.asp?progid=57.

[9] F. W. Lanchester. *Aircraft in Warfare: The Dawn of the Fourth Arm.* London, Constable and Co, Ltd., 1916.

[10] M. K. Lauren and R. T. Stephen. Map-Aware Non-uniform Automata (MANA)—A New Zealand Approach to Scenario Modelling. *Journal of Battlefield Technology*, 5(1 (March)):27ff, 2002. http://www.argospress.com/jbt/Volume5/5-1-4.htm.

[11] R. Marinier and J. Laird. Toward a Comprehensive Computational Model of Emotions and Feelings. In *Proceedings of Sixth International Conference on Cognitive Modeling*, Pittsburgh, PA, pages 172-177, Lawrence Earlbaum, 2004.

[12] R. R. Murphy, C. L. Lisetti, R. Tardif, L. Irish, and A. Gage. Emotion-Based Control of Cooperating Heterogeneous Mobile Robots. *IEEE Transactions on Robotics and Automation*, 18(5 (October)):744-757, 2002.

[13] A. Ortony, G. L. Clore, and A. Collins. *The cognitive structure of emotions.* Cambridge, UK, Cambridge University Press, 1988.

[14] H. V. D. Parunak and S. Brueckner. Modeling Uncertain Domains with Polyagents. In *Proceedings of International Joint Conference on Autonomous Agents and Multi-Agent Systems (AAMAS06)*, Hakodate, Japan, 2006. http://www.altarum.net/~vparunak/AAAMAS06Polyagents.pdf.

[15] H. V. D. Parunak, S. Brueckner, R. Matthews, J. Sauter, and S. Brophy. Characterizing and Predicting Agents via Multi-Agent Evolution. Altarum Institute, Ann Arbor, MI, 2005. http://www.altarum.net/~vparunak/BEE.pdf.

[16] H. V. D. Parunak, S. Brueckner, and R. Savit. Universality in Multi-Agent Systems. In *Proceedings of Third International Joint Conference on Autonomous Agents and Multi-Agent Systems (AAMAS 2004)*, New York, NY, pages 930-937, IEEE, 2004. http://www.altarum.net/~vparunak/AAMAS04Universality.pdf.

[17] H. V. D. Parunak, S. A. Brueckner, R. Matthews, and J. Sauter. Pheromone Learning for Self-Organizing Agents. *IEEE SMC*, 35(3 (May)):316-326, 2005. http://www.altarum.net/~vparunak/ParunakIEEE.pdf.

[18] R. W. Picard. *Affective Computing*. Cambridge, MA, MIT Press, 2000.

[19] A. S. Rao and M. P. Georgeff. Modeling Rational Agents within a BDI Architecture. In *Proceedings of International Conference on Principles of Knowledge Representation and Reasoning (KR-91)*, pages 473-484, Morgan Kaufman, 1991.

[20] C. von Clausewitz. *Vom Kriege*. Berlin, Dümmlers Verlag, 1832.

[21] J. von Neumann. Zur Theorie der Gesellschaftsspiele. *Mathematische Annalen*, 100:295-320, 1928.

[22] J. von Neumann and O. Morgenstern. *Theory of Games and Economic Behavior*. Princeton, Princeton University Press, 1944.

Application of Action Selection, Information Gathering, and Information Evaluation Technologies to UAV Target Tracking

David C. Han, Jisun Park, Karen Fullam, and K. Suzanne Barber

The Laboratory for Intelligent Processes and Systems,
Electrical and Computer Engineering Department,
The University of Texas at Austin
{dhan, jisun, kfullam, barber}@lips.utexas.edu

Abstract. This paper illustrates agent technologies applied to unmanned aerial vehicle (UAV) target tracking. The combination of the three technologies presented in this paper provide UAVs with functionality needed for coordinated autonomous operation, from building up accurate beliefs, efficiently gathering information, to acting rationally. In the UAV target tracking domain, communication among agents is necessary for building beliefs about target locations. Reliable information provisioning networks are constructed through selection of appropriate information sources and trust evaluations are applied to belief revision. Also, a macro-based action selection scheme is deployed for efficient coordination of the target tracking activity among agents.

1 Introduction

Dynamic and unexpected events are the defining characteristics of numerous application domains. These environments often require decision-makers to solve many problems with insufficient resources and time. In the Unmanned Aerial Vehicle (UAV) target tracking domain, numerous UAVs continually collect and deliver location information about moving enemy targets to a tactical operation center (Central Command). UAVs must coordinate with each other to divide tracking responsibilities since uncoordinated execution of tracking activity among UAVs may result in inefficient resource usage. Second, the Central Command must decide which UAVs are the most appropriate information providers of the target locations. Finally, target location information may be inaccurate, perhaps due to sensor failure, noise caused by target movement, or communication delays. Therefore, the operations center must gauge the accuracy of incoming information. These challenges provide an appropriate environment for multi-agent system deployment. Agent technologies proposed in this research provide novel capabilities for (1) coordinating the tracking of multiple targets among a set of UAVs, (2) identifying the best subset of assigned UAVs from which to collect location information, and (3) evaluating the accuracy of location information. These capabilities aid the efficient and effective collection and verification of target location information.

S.G. Thompson and R. Ghanea-Hercock (Eds.): DAMAS 2005 , LNAI 3890, pp. 66–79, 2006.

Section 2 provides an overview of technical details for each technology, followed by descriptions of the UAV target tracking simulation in Section 3. Section 4 summarizes and concludes the paper.

2   Overview of Technical Details

Fig. 1 describes the overall picture of target tracking activities by both UAVs and the Central Command. The scenario captured in Fig. 1 was developed as part of the DARPA Taskable Agent Software Kit (TASK) program in cooperation with the Institute of Advanced Technology and the University XXI program at Fort Hood. Three main technologies deployed in this target tracking domain are explained in the following sections. A number of targets are located on the battlefield (bottom of Fig. 1). Each individual UAV (center) selects some subset of the targets to collect information on. Coordination among the UAVs during target selection improves the efficiency of the tracking operations. The sensor data from the UAVs is sent to the Central Command (top) which forms a unified situational picture.

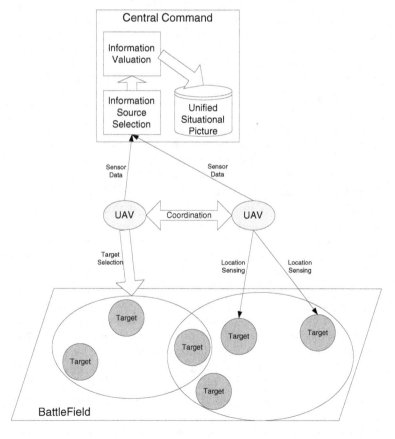

Fig. 1. UAV Target Tracking Domain

2.1   Autonomous Action Selection

Using the model it has for the environment, an agent must decide what actions to perform (e.g., which targets to track in Fig. 1) to affect the environment according to the desires the agent holds. When faced with complex desires (i.e., multiple targets of varying importance), an important characteristic of an autonomous agent is the ability to decide which goals (targets) to pursue and in what order. Markov Decision Processes (MDP) calculate the value of an action as the expected value to be received immediately and in the future through continued rational action. The reward structure for MDPs is limiting since, if the agent has multiple goals to achieve, those goals must be represented as part of the state definition. This research separates the idea of desire states and domain states to enable reasoning at various abstraction levels. For example, the domain states are defined as a product of state variables, $S_{domain} = V_1 \times V_2 \times \cdots \times V_L$. Using each target as a goal, desire states of an agent can be defined as a product of the goal variables (boolean values indicating whether each goal has been achieved), $S_{desire} = G_1 \times G_2 \times \cdots \times G_K$. The states represented in an MDP must be able to differentiate between the same domain state under differing desire states, hence the total space for action selection is the cross product of the domain and desire spaces, $S = V_1 \times V_2 \times \cdots \times V_L \times G_1 \times G_2 \times \cdots \times G_K$. Macro actions are combinations of primitive actions whose execution will lead to specific domain states of interest. Macro actions can be used to separate (factor) analysis of the domain characteristics from analysis of the desires, allowing reuse of the domain analysis when desires change. Lane and Kaelbling have used macro actions to transform MDPs into traveling salesman problems [1]. Action selection can then be performed in terms of desire states. The expected costs of macro execution relate the various desire states to each other, forming the desire space. The motivations for reasoning in the desire space include: (1) the desire space is smaller than the complete state space (the desire space grows only in the number of tasks), and (2) the structure of the desire space can be exploited algorithmically during computation. Full details on this method can be found in [2].

The model for reasoning in the desire space is defined as follows. Given the domain space of the problem S_{domain}, some subset of those states are marked as goals, $G \subseteq S_{domain} = \{g_1, g_2, \ldots, g_K\}$. The states of the desire space are built from the goal variables and the agent's location in the domain space. Each macro action is constructed to move the agent to a respective goal state. The desire states are denoted by a tuple $\langle G_{unach}, s \rangle$. The first element of the tuple, G_{unach} is the set of unachieved goals in that desire state. The second element of the tuple is the location of the agent, $s \in S_{domain}$. The agent can only be located at the initial location $s_{initial}$, or as a result of executing a macro action, in an accomplished goal location g_i, hence, $S_{desire} = \{\langle G, s_{initial} \rangle, \langle G_{unach}, g_i \rangle$ s.t. $G_{unach} \subseteq G$ and $g_i \in G/G_{unach}\}$. The action set $A_{desire} = \{macro_1, macro_2, \ldots, macro_K\}$ is the set of macro actions, one for achieving each goal the agent holds. An action level cost function c_{action} is required to estimate the costs incurred by executing the macro action. This cost is related to the distance the agent must travel from a given domain state to the termination state of the macro. The value of a state is simply the sum of the cost of executing the macro from that state ($c < 0$), the reward for achieving the immediate goal through macro execution, and any expected value for being in the resulting state due to expected future goal achievement. Since goals, once completed, cannot be undone in this domain, loops cannot exist in the graph. This enables calculation of the expected values to proceed through simple accumulation of the values through graph traversal rather than an iterative process (e.g., policy or value iteration).

When multiple agents interact, the concept of task allocation comes into play. An agent is assigned goals by its commander (i.e., the person who deployed the autonomous agent). In the system, the overall set of goals is defined as the union of the individual agents' tasks. If an agent is strictly operating independently from other agents, it only needs to calculate the values for its own set of goals. Interaction with other agents changes the goal evaluation model by either changing the allocation of goals among the agents or by changing the values associated with the constituent goals. Using the evaluations performed above, agents can perform "what-if" evaluations for possible new goal allocations. After task allocations are completed, goal addition, removal, and modification algorithms are used to update the desire-space model to reflect the information about other agents' actions. Interactions with other agents also aid each agent in managing its action selection reasoning by reducing the size of the desire space they consider.

Once the UAV agents decide which targets to track based on the allocated goals and send the sensed location information of the corresponding targets to the Central Command, Central Command must distinguish which UAVs are the "best" target information providers, as described in Section 2.2. This research assumes the system is composed of a large number of UAVs, providing Central Command with options to choose from.

2.2   Selecting Target Information Providers

For a large, dynamic system, Central Command's task of determining which UAVs (agents) to use as information providers can be very challenging. Agents are goal-driven entities and efficient and accurate information acquisition is critical to the agents' goal achievement [3]. In open environments, information sources can come and go, and the unknown quality of information sources varies, resulting in uncertain, untrustworthy information. Dynamic environments result in unreliable information quality, unpredictable changes in network topology, and changes in information requirements. Selecting the appropriate information sources (UAVs) requires the Central Command to decide "from whom to request what", and involves two tasks; search space construction and search. The search space represents the potential sets of information providers accompanied by their evaluations. The challenge comes from the fact that the number of information source combinations increases exponentially as the diversity of information requirements and the number of sources meeting those requirements increase. A proposed heuristic search called hill-climbing with mutation operation explores the search space efficiently and finds the best solution while minimizing the possibility of local optima [4].

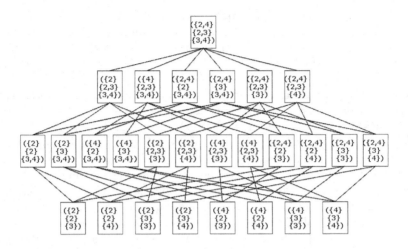

Fig. 2. Information Combination Pool as Search Space

The search space (Fig. 2) consists of a set of nodes representing potential information source combinations. Each instance of an information source combination constitutes a node in a search space and is represented by an M-tuple when an agent requires M types of information [4]. Each element in the M-tuple is a set of information sources corresponding to each information requirement. For example, in $\langle \{a_2, a_4\}, \{a_2\}, \{a_4\} \rangle$, the first requirement is satisfied by a_2 and a_4, the second requirement is satisfied by a_2, and so on. The search space is constructed as a graph called the Information Source Combinations Pool (ICP), shown in Fig. 2, where connected nodes can be mapped into one by adding or removing a single source for a single requirement, so that the adjacent nodes are minimally different. For example, there is an edge between $\langle \{a_2, a_4\}, \{a_2, a_3\}, \{a_3, a_4\} \rangle$ and $\langle \{a_2\}, \{a_2, a_3\}, \{a_3, a_4\} \rangle$, matching the addition or removal source a_4 for the first information requirement (assuming a_4 can provide that information requirement).

The valuation of each ICP node represents how good an information source combination is in terms of trustworthiness, coverage, and cost [4]. Trustworthiness of an information source is represented by the probability distribution of the error of the provided information from the estimate true value [5]. Coverage represents the contribution of the information sources to an agent's goal achievement. Cost is derived from the message-passing and computational burden required to communicate information. The currently selected node is intended to be the best source combination at the current time. Information sources are replaced when new combinations (1) including better partners, (2) excluding bad or (3) be an almost or completely new set of information sources having a higher evaluation value than the current ones do. In the case of (1) and (2), it is likely that most of the current partners are still included. Therefore, it is desirable to keep the search path near the current node because it is likely that a better node exists near the current node. Single source changes (edges) in the ICP let an agent make use of the locality of the search space during exploration. However, depending only on the locality can reach a local optimum or can slow down the search in the case of (3), so exploration of the search space must be expanded to reduce the possibility of the local optimum. However, expanding the exploration in turn costs more and may waste the resource if the exploration does not return a better result.

Hill-climbing with mutation operation concurrently make use both of the locality by adopting hill climbing search method [6] and of the exploration by adopting a mutation operation borrowed from genetic algorithms [7]. Hill-climbing is a heuristic search seeking a state which is better than the current state, and thus we can always get a result which is better than or at least equal to the current state. Mutation serves to generate a new node to be inspected by applying a simple modification rule to the current node, and it enables random walks in the search to detect a local optimum and helps escape from the local optimum.

Once Central Command has decided from which UAVs to request which information, it must valuate the incoming information to build an accurate estimate of target location, as demonstrated in Section 2.3.

2.3   Valuation of Target Location Information

After Central Command has identified potential tracking UAVs for a given target, as explained in Section 2.2, it must then select the best location information from those UAVs; some information may not be reliable due to sensor inaccuracies, noise, or age. By adopting a set of policies for choosing information, Central Command can attempt to minimize the risks associated with dependencies on information-providing UAVs (as dynamics in agent capability and environmental conditions introduce change).

Since Central Command does not know true target locations, it has no basis to judge the quality of information based on a UAV's communicated values alone. However, it can follow general policies [5] for identifying the most accurate information. These policies, identified below, are naïve heuristics when implemented in isolation. For example, Jonker and Treur [8], Sen and Sajja [9], and Yu and Singh [10] have developed mechanisms for modeling source trustworthiness (see #4 below), but their modeling fails to consider that reliable sources may have uncertain or expired information. An algorithm employing a compromise of all policies can identify robustly the most valuable information for good decision-making.

1. *Priority of Maximum Information:* When forming an estimate, incorporate information from as many UAVs as possible. Based on the Central Limit Theorem, given information from a greater number of UAVs, the derived

estimate should be closer to the trust value being estimated. This concept works best with many reporting UAVs and assumes that UAVs are statistically independent in their reporting.

2. *Priority to Corroborated Information:* Give priority to information that can be corroborated. High value should be assigned to information that is similar to other information.

3. *Priority for Source Certainty:* Give priority to information from UAVs conveying high certainty on that information. If the UAV is proficient at conveying a quality certainty assessment, that certainty assessment will be an indication of the accuracy of the information.

4. *Priority to Reliable Sources:* Give priority to information from UAVs estimated to be most reliable. If a reporting UAV is estimated to be a provider of quality information (in other words, the UAV has a high reputation), based on past experience or recommendations from other entities, then the information provided by that UAV should have high value.

5. *Priority to Recent Information:* Give priority to information estimated to be most recent. Since the true target location being estimated is more likely to have changed as more time passes, older information is less likely to be accurate. In order to assign relative value to information of different ages, the rate at which the target location changes must be known; the faster that location changes, the more quickly information loses value.

These five policies can ensure secure decision-making despite uncertainty in source information by acknowledging three types of error in source-reported information. First, error may be due to the age of the information. As discussed previously, the target location being estimated may have changed since the information was received, and we assume the amount of change is related to the amount of time that has passed. Second, error may be due to UAV unreliability. UAVs may be malicious (taken over by the enemy) or incompetent (due to sensor failure). Third, error may be due to the UAV's uncertainty in its information. A UAV may be uncertain about the information it provides due to the uncertain quality of its own sensors or the age of its own information, for example. In the algorithm we employ, UAVs communicating greater certainty experience greater loss or benefit to their reputations. Therefore, UAVs have an incentive to accurately communicate their certainty on the information they provide. Because UAVs are permitted to convey their own certainty in their reports, Central Command is relieved from evaluating the "history" of the information prior to its receipt by Central Command itself. For example, Central Command need not care about the age of the data from the UAV's perspective or the quality of the UAV's sensors; those factors should be expressed in the UAV's certainty conveyed to Central Command.

3   Application to UAV Target Tracking

The technologies described in Section 2 have been implemented in a simulation of UAV target tracking for the purposes of experimentation and demonstration. In this simulation, targets are located at various points in a 2-dimensional surveillance field and agents, controlling UAVs, track target locations. Fig. 3 shows the graphical user interface for the demonstration of action selection. Each UAV is represented by a dot surrounded by a circle indicating the UAV's sensor radius. Targets are depicted by dots surrounded by shaded circles whose size and darkness represent the amount of time elapsed since the target sensed by any UAV. The scenario for this simulation assumes a Central Command receives target location information from UAV agents and forms estimates about target locations. UAV agents have varying reliability depending on sensor quality.

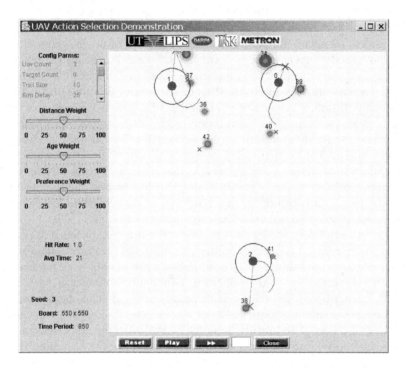

Fig. 3. Simulation demonstration coordination among UAVs for multiple moving targets

At the most basic level, an agent has control over the heading and speed of a single UAV. A state in the state space is defined by the location, heading, and speed of the UAV in conjunction with the locations of the targets. Each target has an associated reward value, which grows with the urgency of that target (i.e., the time since last scanned). Movement incurs a cost proportional to the distance traveled as an abstraction of resources, such as fuel, forcing the agents to trade off expected rewards against costs.

Each agent is charged with selecting which target their UAV is going to service next with the overall goal of keeping the models of target positions updated. Towards this end, target valuations are guided by two principles: (1) the desire to service a particular target is increases as time passes, and (2) the desire to service a particular target decreases as distance to that target increases. The first principle is ensures fairness, so that all targets will eventually be serviced. The second principle increases the efficiency of the servicing, encouraging the agents to service nearby targets first, rather than crisscrossing the space. Target movements introduce uncertainty into value estimation. Calculating the exact expected cost incurred by an agent to reach a given target is rather complex due to this uncertainty but a probabilistic encounter model could be used, estimating cost as a function of the distance between the UAV and the target).

Action of the UAVs also adds uncertainty to modeling the expected reward value for visiting a target. Visiting a recently visited target is less useful to keeping an up-to-date situational picture than updating information on older targets. Unless an agent can predict the future actions of other agents, an agent is not guaranteed to receive any reward for its work. For coordination, agents communicate some aspects of their internal decision-making evaluations. For example, the agents may communicate their exact desire valuations on the targets, or after computation, a preference relation describing their valuations in a more general manner (revealing less information to the other agents). Additionally, if an agent is committed to performing an action, it will eventually perform that action unless rendered incapable. Upon receipt of any of these communications, agents update their desire space models (as described in Section 2.1) to recalculate the most rational course of action. Using this framework, the simulation was used to compare four coordination mechanisms: no coordination, location-based inference, communicated inference, and explicit partitioning.

With no coordination, the agents operate without any knowledge of the other agents in the system. This option requires no additional computational resources or communication on behalf of the agents. Since the agents have no awareness of the other agents, they tend to operate redundantly, often visiting the same targets. Location-based inference and communicated inference both spread the UAVs through an implicit partitioning of the targets, discounting the expected rewards based on predicted future behavior of the other agents. Location-based inference uses only location information for the other UAVs. Assuming that the UAV will service nearby targets, targets that are closer to other agents have their expected rewards reduced in the desire-space. Communicated inference is similar to location-based inference, but the agents calculate which are their preferred targets and communicate those preferences to the other agents. The benefit of this approach over location-based inference is that the agents can incorporate their local knowledge when calculating their preferences.

With explicit partitioning, the agents negotiate an allocation of the goals to respective agents, effectively reducing the overlap to zero through removal of goals from the agents' desire-space models. Possible drawbacks of using explicit partitioning include an increase in communications and computational resources needed to calculate and negotiate the partition. Also, this method, if improperly used, can result in commitments far into the future, restricting the ability to adapt to changing conditions.

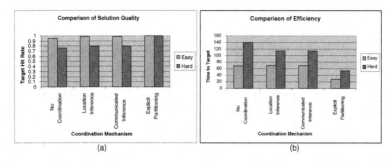

Fig. 4. Results comparing the effect of coordination on action selection in terms of (a) solution quality, and (b) efficiency of action

Fig. 4 compares the four coordination mechanisms described above. In each case, three agents are used to cover a battlefield. Targets are added to random locations on the battlefield at regular intervals. Difficulty of coverage (easy/hard) is related to the speed at which targets are added. Targets have a given lifetime after which they are removed by the mission commander. If this occurs, it is counted as a missed target. Fig. 4(a) shows the effect of the coordination mechanisms on the ability for the agents to spread out across the battlefield. The results show that explicit partitioning is the best, while the implicitly partitioning of location inference and communicated inference are slightly better than no coordination. Fig. 4(b) shows the efficiency of the agents at retrieving their rewards, measuring the distance traveled on average to visit each target since cost is dependent upon distance. Increasing the amount of coordination reduces

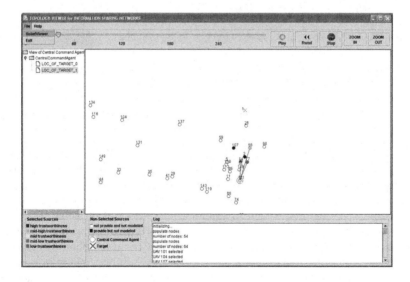

Fig. 5. Topology Viewer demonstrating selection of UAVs as providers of information about target locations

the distance traveled, meaning there was less overlap in the actions of the agents due to less uncertainty about the actions of other agents.

Once the UAVs are in action collecting information about the targets, the Central Command must evaluate that information to form a unified situational picture. Demonstrating the research presented in Section 2.2, Fig. 5 (the Topology Viewer) shows which information sources are selected by the Central Command. The main pane shows the spatial layout of the UAVs in the system. The Central Command is depicted by a dot surrounded by a red circle. Targets of interest are marked by red Xs. Lines from the Central Command indicate which UAVs (information sources) have been selected, with the color of the source indicating their trustworthiness. A legend describing the meaning of the colors is provided in the lower left of the interface. This viewer demonstrates the dynamic information source selection by the Central Command, illustrating changing source selections as time progresses and UAVs and targets move around.

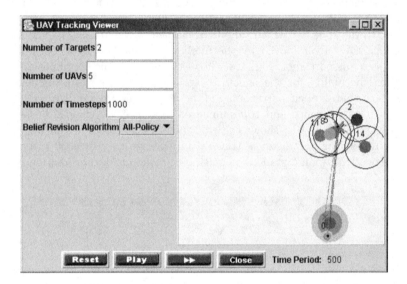

Fig. 6. UAV Simulation demonstrating the All-Policy Algorithm for belief revision

Fig. 6 shows the graphical user interface setting up the belief revision simulation and experiments. In this simulation, a user can set the number of targets, the number of UAVs, the number of timesteps, and a belief revision algorithm. The scenario for this simulation assumes a Central Command which receives reports from UAV agents, which are modeled as information sources, about a target's location each time the source senses the target, (i.e., when the target is within that UAV's sensor range). The Central Command then forms beliefs about target locations. UAV agents have varying reliability depending on their sensors; one UAV Agent may have a sensor that is more accurate than the sensor belonging to another UAV Agent. UAV Agents obtain target location information from their sensors at varying intervals depending on their flight paths.

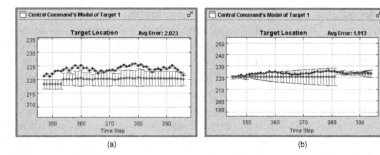

Fig. 7. Target location estimation results comparing (a) Naïve Algorithm and (b) All-Policy Algorithm

Fig. 7 (a) and (b) demonstrate the improvement in location estimate accuracy when information valuation policies are utilized. Fig. 7 (a) shows Central Command's target location estimates as computed using no information valuation (Naïve Algorithm), averaging location information from all UAV agents. Fig. 7 (b) displays Central Command's estimates as computed based on the five policies of Section 2.3, using the All-Policy algorithm for choosing UAV location information. Dots with error bars represent Central Command's estimate of target location and its certainty on that estimate, respectively. For comparison purposes, lone dots represent the target's actual location. First, note that the All-Policy algorithm achieves lower error in its target location estimates, shown both on the chart and by the computed average error. Second, when Central Command is receiving no UAV Agent reports (when the location estimate remains static), the All-Policy algorithm adjusts its error bars to accommodate the known decrease in target location certainty.

4 Conclusions

This paper illustrates three agent technologies applied to the UAV target tracking domain for (1) coordinating target tracking among multiple UAV agents, (2) identifying the UAVs serving as the best information providers, and (3) evaluating the accuracy of location information.

UAV agents try to make the best (rational) decisions they can, to change the domain according to their desires. Computational efficiency, when determining the best action, is improved by using macro actions to factor the state space and estimate the cost of pursuing each goal. Reasoning is performed in the "desire space", which describes the expected value of pursuing a goal in the context of how selected actions facilitate the pursuit of other goals in the future. The desire space also permits evaluation of task allocations, enabling "what-if" reasoning and coordination among the agents.

In the UAV target tracking domain, because of the inherent incompleteness in agents' sensing capability, communication among agents is necessary for building beliefs about target locations. To facilitate the target tracking activity, a reliable information network is constructed by finding the most appropriate information sources (UAVs in this case) from which to acquire necessary target location information. While the exchange of information through the communication can compensate for the lack of complete capability, the agents can be exposed to unexpected degradation of information quality by the communicated information. Therefore, it is critical for agents to be equipped with a capability to distinguish between "good" agents and "bad" agents, and to construct an information sharing network with "good" agents. Good agents acting as information sources are those who are the most trustworthy and provide the most relevant information at the least cost [11]. A heuristic search algorithm based on agent evaluations enables the agents to build the information sharing networks with the appropriate information sources.

Trustworthiness evaluation not only helps in finding appropriate information sources, but also is significant for building accurate beliefs. Beliefs constitute a situational picture about the environment, and may affect the decision-making of agents holding the beliefs. This research uses a policy-based trustworthiness evaluation scheme. This policy-based scheme combines a set of heuristics for information valuation to overcome the potential risks or uncertainty caused by information exchange. The policy-based trustworthiness evaluation can ensure decision-making security.

The combination of these three technologies provides each UAV with functionality needed for coordinated autonomous operation and accurate situational pictures by building partnerships with "good" information sources then dynamically valuating the information from those sources.

Acknowledgements

This research is sponsored in part by the Defense Advanced Research Project Agency (DARPA) Taskable Agent Software Kit (TASK) program, F30602-00-2-0588. The U.S. Government is authorized to reproduce and distribute reprints for Governmental purpose notwithstanding any copyright annotation thereon. The views and conclusions herein are those of the authors and should not be interpreted as necessarily representing the official policies or endorsements, either expressed or implied, of the Defense Advanced Research Project Agency.

References

1. Lane, T., Kaelbling, L.P.: Nearly deterministic abstractions of markov decision processes. In: Eighteenth National Conference on Artificial Intelligence (AAAI2002), Edmonton, Alberta, Canada (2002) 260–266
2. Han, D.C., Barber, K.S.: Desire-space analysis and action selection for multiple, dynamic goals. In Leite, João, Torrono, P., eds.: Compuational Logic in Multi-Agent Systems. LNAI 3487, Springer-Verlag (2005) 249–264
3. Castelfranchi, C.: Guarantees for autonomy in cognitive agent architecture. In Wooldridge, M.J., Jennings, N.R., eds.: Intelligent Agents: ECAI-94 Workshop on Agents, Theories, Architectures, and Languages, Springer-Verlag (1995) 56–70

4. Park, J., Barber, K.S.: Information quality assurance by lazy exploration of information sources combination space in open multi-agent systems. Journal of Universal Computer Science **11** (2005) 193–209

5. Fullam, K., Barber, K.S.: Using policies for information valuation to justify beliefs. In: Proceedings of the Third International Conference on Autonomous and Multi-Agent Systems (AAMAS 2004), New York City, New York (2004) 404–411

6. Russell, S., Norvig, P.: Artificial Intelligence: A Modern Approach. Prentice Hall, Englewood Cliffs, New Jersey (1995)

7. Holland, J.H.: Adaptation in Natural and Artificial Systems. The University of Michigan Press, Ann Arbor, Michigan (1975)

8. Jonker, C.M., Treur, J.: Formal analysis of models for the dynamics of trust based experiences. In: Proceedings of 9th European Workshop on Modelling Autonomous Agents in a Multi-Agent World : Multi-Agent System Engineering. (1999) 221–232

9. Sen, S., Sajja, N.: Robustness of reputation-based trust: Boolean case. In: Proceedings of the First International Joint Conference on Autonomous Agents and Multiagent Systems, Bologna, Italy (2002) 288–293

10. Yu, B., P., S.M.: An evidential model of distributed reputation management. In: Proceedings of The First International Joint Conference on Autonomous Agents and Multiagent Systems, Bologna, Italy (2002) 294–301

11. Barber, K.S., Park, J.: Agent belief autonomy in open multi-agent systems. In: Agents and Computational Autonomy: Potential, Risks, and Solutions. LNCS 2969, Springer-Verlag (2004) 7–16

A Multi-agent UAV Swarm
for Automatic Target Recognition

Prithviraj Dasgupta[1], Stephen O'Hara[1], and Plamen Petrov[2]

[1] Department of Computer Science,
University of Nebraska, Omaha, NE 68182
[2] 21st Century Systems Inc., Omaha, NE 68182

Abstract. We address the problem of automatic target recognition (ATR) using a multi-agent swarm of unmanned aerial vehicles(UAVs) deployed within a reconnaissance area. Traditionally, ATR is performed by UAVs that fly within the reconnaissance area to collect image data through sensors and upload the data to a central base station for analyzing and identifying potential targets. The centralized approach to ATR introduces several problems including scalability with the number of UAVs, network delays in communicating with the central location, and, susceptibility of the system to malicious attacks on the central location. In this paper, we describe a multi-agent system of UAVs to perform ATR. We assume that each UAV has limited computational capabilities and target identification can be performed by several UAVs that combine their resources including their computational capabilities. The UAVs employ a swarming algorithm implemented through software agents to congregate at and identify potential targets, and, a gossiping mechanism to disseminate information within the swarm.

1   Introduction

Automatic target recognition (ATR) involves determining the visual and other distinguishing features (signature) of an object, usually from a distance, and using this signature to automatically identify the object as a potential target. Over the last few years, unmanned aerial vehicles(UAVs) have been employed to obtain image data through their sensors from objects within a reconnaissance area. This image data is uploaded to a central location, usually the base station, where potential targets are identified using image classification and identification algorithms [2, 6, 8]. The base station has considerable computing resources and is capable of fusing the data obtained from the multiple UAV sensors to perform intelligent image classification. However, this centralized model for ATR introduces several problems including scalability with the number of UAVs, network delays in communicating with the central location, and, susceptibility of the system to malicious attacks on the central location.

With the advancement of technology, the computation power of processors on UAVs has improved significantly and mini-UAVs can perform moderate computation beyond the trivial data acquisition and upload to a central processing

S.G. Thompson and R. Ghanea-Hercock (Eds.): DAMAS 2005 , LNAI 3890, pp. 80–91, 2006.

location. In contrast to a centralized model for ATR, we envisage that the computing power of individual UAVs could be assimilated into a swarm of coordinating UAVs that perform ATR in a distributed manner. In a swarmed model, each UAV individually searches for potential targets within an area of interest using its image sensor. As soon as the image of an object is sensed to be a possible target by a UAV, other UAVs cooperate with it by swarming towards the potential target to collectively perform ATR and confirm the object as a target. A distributed model for ATR can scale with the number of UAVs, and, is also less susceptible to communication delays and security attacks than the centralized model. Therefore, it makes sense to investigate a distributed computation model for ATR. In this paper, we describe a multi-agent system called COMSTAR(Co-Operative Multi-agent Swarm for automatic TArget Recognition) that enables a group of UAVs deployed within a reconnaissance area to behave collectively as a swarm and perform ATR in a distributed manner. In contrast to traditional distributed processing techniques used for implementing decentralized algorithms, we have employed an ant based algorithm to implement the swarming behavior of our system.

2 Ant-Based Swarming Algorithm for ATR

Our swarming mechanism for ATR is inspired by the *stigmergetic* activity used by social insects such as ants [1] to locate food. Stigmergy enables ants to indirectly communicate with each other about their environment using a chemical substance called pheromone. For example, while searching for food ants start from their nest and leave behind a pheromone trail along the path they traverse. The path from the nest leading to a food receives the highest amount of pheromone. Pheromone provides positive reinforcement to future ants, and, ants searching for the food later on use the trail as a positive reinforcement to lead themselves to the food.

To enable the ant algorithm in our system, we use pheromone to indicate potential targets while ants are implemented through software agents located within the computers on the UAVs. Software agents are characterized by a small footprint (few kilobytes) and are suitable for execution on computers within UAVs with limited computation power.

The problem of ATR by UAVs is different from the stigmergetic behavior of ants. In the traditional ant algorithm, ants leave a pheromone trail on the ground over which they travel. However, for airborne UAVs there is no physical medium through which the pheromone can be communicated with each other. Also, because the model is distributed with computation being performed locally by each UAV, shared memory based techniques cannot be used to communicate pheromone. Here, we have used a gossip based mechanism to enabled stigmergetic communication between UAVs. In the traditional ant algorithm, the food that needs to be discovered by ants is assumed to be available at a fixed location. However, in ATR the location of a mobile target(e.g. tank) can vary temporally. In our algorithm, we have used subtractive anti-pheromone to dynamically update rapidly changing trails corresponding to mobile targets. Finally, in traditional ant algorithms, ants explore or *forage* the region using a random walk when no pheromone trail is available. However, random foraging cannot be used for UAVs because UAVs might collide with each other while moving randomly, or, a UAV might end up repeatedly flying over an area that has already been analyzed by itself or other UAVs. In this paper, we use a deterministic foraging mechanism that enables UAVs to disperse away from each other to avoid collision and redundant analyses of ground areas in the absence of pheromone information. In the next section, we describe the operation of the COMSTAR system and then we describe the modified ant algorithm that enables swarming behavior among the UAVs in COMSTAR.

3   COMSTAR Operation

We consider a battlefield scenario where commanders(humans) located at the base station are interested in detecting potential targets within a reconnaissance area. To achieve this, UAVs are deployed from the base station into the area of interest(AOI). Because the AOI can be considerably large in size and might contain areas with geographical features that are not navigable by UAVs (for e.g., mountains, corridors) the AOI is logically divided into smaller sub-areas and a group of UAVs is deployed by the base station into each of these sub-areas. The number of UAVs comprising a UAV-group is determined by equally dividing the total number of UAVs at the base station over the number of sub-areas within the AOI. The sub-area within which a UAV is deployed by the base station is referred to as the home area of the UAV. UAV's can leave their home area to visit other regions of the AOI to manifest the swarming behavior of the system. Because our focus in this paper is the swarming behavior of the system, we assume that the algorithm for determining the geometry and number of the sub-areas is available at the base station and we do not discuss this problem further in this paper.

We assume that each UAV is provided with the following equipment to enable it to perform ATR: (1) Wireless communication capability for sending and receiving messages from other UAVs and the base station. (2) One or more image sensors capable of capturing snapshots of the area over which the UAV flies. (3) Processor with limited computing capability. (4) Rudimentary image processing software that enables the UAV to identify objects obtained by its image sensors as potential targets. We assume image processing algorithms for ATR [7] are available for incorporation on a UAV and concentrate on the swarming behavior of the system in the rest of the paper. (5) A global positioning system(GPS) that returns the 3-d co-ordinates (latitude, longitude, altitude) of the UAV's current location.

Because of limited computational resources available on a single UAV, we assume that a UAV's image processing algorithm is not sophisticated enough to definitely identify an object as a target. For definite target identification, n other UAVs need to visit the location of the potential target to observe and confirm it as a definitive target. The swarming behavior in the system becomes more pronounced as n increases. The exact value of n can be determined by the base station from the operational requirements and constraints of a specific battlefield scenario.

3.1   UAV Operation

After being deployed within its home-area, each UAV uses the deterministic foraging algorithm described in Section 4.1 to navigate within its home area. The UAV's image sensor continuously captures snapshots of objects within its viewing area and passes them to the image processing algorithm. When the UAV's image processing algorithm determines an object sensed by it as a potential target, it has to enlist the cooperation of n other UAVs to confirm the potential target. To enable this, when a UAV discovers a potential target it associates a particular amount of pheromone with the location of the potential target. Pheromone decays with time. The pheromone value of the potential target is broadcast over the UAV's wireless communication link using a gossip mechanism described in 4.3. UAVs that are within the communication range of the broadcasting UAV receive the gossiped pheromone value, and, also forward it to other UAVs.

Because there are likely to be multiple targets within the AOI, a UAV can receive multiple gossiped pheromone values. The objective of each UAV is to navigate towards the potential target that has the highest time-discounted pheromone value. The overall effect of this behavior would be that most UAVs get attracted towards the most prominent potential target, manifesting in the swarming behavior of the system.

To implement the swarming behavior in our system, each UAV maintains a pheromone landscape containing an abstraction of the potential targets that the UAV is aware of through its sensors, or, through gossip from other UAVs. The goal of each UAV is to move towards the location with the highest time-discounted pheromone value on its pheromone landscape.

In COMSTAR, different UAVs might have different sensor capabilities and image processing algorithms leading to different perceptions(pheromone value) for the same potential target. If each UAV decides to blindly move towards the most prominent potential target as soon as it hears gossip about it, aborting its current mission and without considering the potential target's time-discounted pheromone value, the differences in perception of different strategic agents, and the time required to reach the target, the UAVs would end up switching goals very rapidly, and, possibly, the swarming behavior of the system would be never be achieved. To address this problem each UAV maintains a prioritized set of tasks, each task corresponding to a point on its pheromone landscape. The decision by a UAV to alter its current mission and pursue a new task(potential target) is based on the priority of the task within its task set.

In the next section, we describe the algorithms used by a UAV to implement the swarming behavior of the system. Because each UAV encapsulates the software agent that implements these algorithms, we use the terms agent and UAV interchangeably in the rest of the paper.

4   Model

We consider a set of $\mathcal{A}$ agents. Each agent $i \in \mathcal{A}$ maintains the following sets:

- Ψ_i: Pheromone landscape of agent i comprising the set of potential targets received through gossip or discovered through its sensors,
- Γ_i: set of tasks corresponding to the targets it is aware of.

Each point ψ in Ψ_i corresponds to a potential target is defined as $\psi = \{pher, loc, time\}$, where $pher \in [0, 1]$ is the amount of pheromone associated with the potential target, $loc \in L \subset \mathcal{R}^3$ is the location of the potential target in 3-d co-ordinates (latitude, longitude, altitude) obtained through the UAV's GPS, and $time$ is the time at which this pheromone was last updated. In COM-STAR, time is measured in logical units called *ticks*. Every entity in COMSTAR receives the current time measured in ticks from a globally available clock (in the COMSTAR simulator)[1].The availability of globally available clock avoids synchronization problems between different UAVs in COMSTAR.

Each task $\gamma \in \Gamma_i$ corresponds to a pheromone-point on the pheromone land-scape Ψ_i of agent i and is defined as $\gamma = \{\psi, prio, status\}$ where $\psi \in \Psi_i$ is the pheromone corresponding to the task, $prio \in [0, 1]$ is the priority of task γ, and, $status = \{Potential, Definite\}$ gives the identification status of the target. The priority of each task $\gamma \in \Gamma_i$ is recalculated every time the pheromone landscape of agent i gets updated. Each UAV has limited computational resources includ-ing data storage capacity. Therefore, we assume that each agent can hold a finite number of tasks within its task set and discards low priority tasks that cannot fit within the storage limits of the task set.

An agent's set of actions is given by:

- *Navigate* to the location of the highest priority task within its task set
- *Gossip* pheromone values that it is aware of
- *Forage* deterministically to explore the AOI when the task set is empty.

4.1   Deterministic Foraging

The task set Γ_i of agent i is empty when it is initially deployed within its home area by the base station, and, when there is no gossiped pheromone information that are attractive enough for the agent to move towards. In such a scenario, agent i forages on its own using the deterministic foraging algorithm, as shown in Figure 1. The deterministic foraging algorithm divides the immediate vicinity of an agent into sectors and then selects the least dense sector to move to. This ensures that while foraging agents maintain sufficient distance with each other so that they do not physically collide with each other, or, perform repeated surveillance of the same area that has no potential targets.

---

[1] In a real battlefield scenario, the current time can be obtained by each UAV from its GPS.

```
Location deterministicForage(){
    Agent[] agentList;
    int[] agentsInSectors; // number of agents in sector j
    agentList = getNearbyAgentList(); //using ping responses
    for each agent a in agentList
        Determine sector containing a and update count
                agentsInSector for that sector;
        Select the sector that has the least value of agentsInSector;
        return the 3-d co-ordinates of midpoint of selected sector
}
```

Fig. 1. Deterministic foraging algorithm used by agent i

4.2 Pheromone Landscape Update

The pheromone landscape ψ_i of agent i gets updated when it receives new pheromone information through gossip from other UAVs, or discovers a potential target through its sensors. The equations used for pheromone update are:

$$\psi.pher_{new} = \lambda\psi.pher_{old} + (1 - \lambda)pher_{in} \tag{1}$$

where, $\psi.pher_{new}$ denotes the updated pheromone level, ψ_{in} denotes the incoming pheromone information from gossip or direct sensing of a potential target by a UAV, and $\psi.pher_{old}$ denotes the time-discounted value of the pheromone level of the pheromone-point ψ, if the point was already there on agent i's pheromone landscape. $\psi.pher_{old} = 0$ if the pheromone-point did not exist in agent i's pheromone landscape. The parameter λ in Equation 1 controls the preference between newly received pheromone information and prior information of a pheromone point corresponding to a potential target. The parameter $\psi.pher_{in}$ in Equation 1 is calculated as:

$$\psi.pher_{in} = \begin{cases} w_1s + w_2c & \text{(when target is directly sensed by UAV)} \\ \psi'.pher. & \text{(pher. value obtained through gossip)} \end{cases} \tag{2}$$

The parameters s and c in Equation 2 represent the severity of the potential target and the confidence in identifying the image from the sensor as a potential target. Both these parameters are returned by the UAV's image processing algorithm. Weights w_1 and w_2 represent agent i's belief in the parameters s and c. Similar to Equation 2, the parameters $\psi.loc$ and $\psi.time$ for pheromone point ψ are updated with the current location and time when a potential target is directly sensed by a UAV, or, updated with the corresponding location and time values obtained through the gossiped pheromone information otherwise.

Pheromone values are time-discounted. Therefore, the actual value of pheromone $\psi.pher$ perceived by an agent is given by:

$$\psi.pher_{actual} = \psi.pher.e^{-\beta(currentTime-\psi.time)},$$

where β is a control parameter.

4.3 Gossip Mechanism

Each agent employs a gossip mechanism [9] to communicate with other agents. For this, an agent first broadcasts a *ping* message. Other agents that are within communication range of the agent originating the ping message respond with a *ping-ack* message that sets up the wireless communication channel between the sender and receiver agents. An agent sends out a ping message at intervals of t_{ping} given by:

$$t_{ping} = u * gossipDelay$$

where, $u \in (0, 1]$ denotes the urgency of agent i to gossip with other agents and *gossipDelay* denotes the maximum allowable interval between two gossips. The algorithm for gossip used by agents is outlined in Figure 2.

```
void gossip(){
        // First send gossip to all agents(UAVs) within comm-range
        Broadcast ping message
        a = set of agents that responded with a ping − ack
        for each element ψ ∈ Ψᵢ
            sendMessage(ψ, a);

        // Receive gossip from other UAVs
        Queue gossipInQueue;
        gossipInQueue = Get messages gossiped by other agents
        for each element q in gossipQueue {
            ψ' = q.getPheromonePoint();
            // check to see if information on pheromone point ψ
            // is already there in agent i's pheromone landscape
            if ∃ψ''.loc ∈ Ψᵢ satisfying (ψ'.loc = ψ''.loc){
                    Update ψ''.pher, ψ''.time in Ψᵢ using Equation 1
                    Update γ.prio for task γ that has γ.ψ.loc = ψ'.loc
                        using Equation 3
            }
            else{ // add ψ' to Ψᵢ
                    Ψᵢ = Ψᵢ ∪ ψ';
                    Create a new task γ in Γᵢ
                        γ.prio is calculated using Equation 3
                        γ.ψ = ψ'
                        γ.status = Potential
        }}}
```

Fig. 2. Gossip algorithm used by an agent

4.4 Task Prioritization and Navigation

The pheromone landscape Ψ_i and corresponding task set Γ_i of agent i gets updated as agent i becomes aware of new potential targets. Agent i uses its decision function $\mathcal{D}_i : \Gamma_i \to L$, where $L \subset \mathcal{R}^3$ to determine the location corresponding to the highest priority task in its task set Γ_i.

$$\mathcal{D}_i(\Gamma_i) = L,$$

where $L = \gamma'.loc$, and, $\gamma' = arg\ max_{\gamma.prio,\ \gamma \in \Gamma_i}\ \Gamma_i$.

The priority of each task $\gamma \in \Gamma_i$ is dynamically calculated based on the agent i's current task (i.e., its current destination), its current location, and the distance and direction of the potential target corresponding to task γ with respect to the the current location and current destination of agent i.

The priority function $prio : \gamma.\psi \times \gamma_{dest}.\psi \times l_c \times l_d \to [0,1]$ where $\gamma.\psi \in [0,1]$ is the amount of pheromone associated with task(target) γ, $\gamma_{dest}.\psi \in [0,1]$ is the amount of pheromone associated with the current destination of agent i, and $l_c, l_d, \in L \subset \mathcal{R}^3$ are the co-ordinates of the current location of the agent, and the co-ordinates of the agent's current destination respectively. We have defined the priority function as:

$$prio = \frac{\gamma.\psi}{\gamma_{dest}.\psi} \times \chi,$$
$$\chi = ((tcb + tdb)(\mid l_\gamma - l_c \mid) + \mid l_d - l_c \mid)^\mu \qquad (3)$$

where χ represents the amount of travel saved by visiting the pheromone-point corresponding to task γ before the destination, μ is a control parameter, and $tcb, tdb \in \{1, -1\}$ are variables that represent the current bearing of the target with respect to agent i's current location and current destination respectively. This definition of the priority function ensures that pheromone-points that are significantly prominent than agent i's current destination, or, are en-route to agent i's current destination receive a higher priority than agent i's current destination. In such a scenario, agent i postpones its current task (current destination) and switches its action to perform (i.e., move towards the location of) the pheromone-point corresponding to task γ.

The navigation algorithm determines the location that the agent has to visit next. This location is determined either by the potential target corresponding to the task with the highest priority in each agent's task set, or, by the deterministic foraging algorithm when the task set is empty. When the UAV's fuel reserves are depleted, the UAV returns to the base station for re-fueling. The navigation algorithm used by agent i is outlined in Figure 3.

After a potential target is identified as a definite target, the pheromone deposits corresponding to it are eliminated from the pheromone landscape of every agent that participated in identifying it. After the target is identified, other agents that do not participate in the target identification stop receiving gossiped pheromone information about the target. The pheromone values about the potential target available on other agents' pheromone landscapes get decayed over time to a zero-value. Therefore, other agents are not attracted to the location where a target has already been identified.

```
void navigate(){
    Location l;
    if (FuelLevelLow = true) moveUAVTo(baseStation);
    else if (Γᵢ = {})
            moveUAVTo(location returned by deterministicForage());
    else{
        for each γ ∈ Γᵢ
            Update the time-discounted priority of γ using Equation 3
        moveUAVTo(𝒟ᵢ(Γᵢ));
    }}
```

Fig. 3. Navigation algorithm used by an agent

4.5   Mobile Targets and Anti-pheromone

Identifying mobile targets for ATR in a distributed swarmed environment is a challenging problem. Mobility of a potential target implies that the pheromone value associated with the position of the potential target is no longer valid when its moves to a new location. Simultaneously, the new location of the target should now have a pheromone value associated with it. The dynamic location of the target would correspond to a specific pheromone value whose location moves dynamically with the target. To enable identification of mobile targets, when a UAV arrives at a location corresponding to a potential target reported through gossip and does not see the target, it deposits anti-pheromone at the location to update (cancel) the pheromone value associated with the location. Anti-pheromone at a location repels UAVs in the future from visiting the location. If the agent is able to detect the potential target at a new location, it also deposits pheromone at the new location of the mobile target. The gossiped pheromone information about the target's new location attracts future UAVs to the target's new location.

5   Simulation Results

We have implemented the COMSTAR system over the AEDGE agent platform that provides a simulation environment for multi-agent systems. In AEDGE, agents corresponding to UAVs and targets can be placed at different geographic locations on a 3-d map. For our first simulation, we consider a scenario comprising six agents(UAVs) employing our swarming algorithm to locate and identify three stationary targets within an AOI. The AOI is divided into three rectangular sub-areas corresponding to the home-areas for each pair of UAVs. As shown in Figure 4, UAVs use the deterministic foraging algorithm when they are initially deployed within their home area because their task set Γ_i is empty. We assume that at least $n = 3$ UAVs are required to confirm a potential target as a definite target. As the information about the potential target gets gossiped by UAVs,

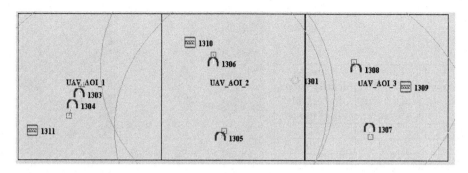

Fig. 4. Snapshot from a COMSTAR simulation illustrating the deterministic foraging behavior of UAVs when they are initially deployed in their home-areas

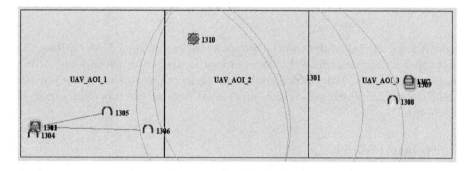

Fig. 5. Snapshot from a COMSTAR simulation illustrating the location of UAVs after a target is identified definitively. UAVs from different locations in the reconnaissance area form a swarm to arrive at and confirm the potential target.

each UAV updates its pheromone landscape and uses its decision function to move towards the most prominent potential target for confirming it as a definite target. Because our scenario comprises only two UAV's per home area, at least one UAV from a different home area must travel towards each potential target to assist in its identification. This swarming behavior of the UAVs is illustrated in Figure 5 that shows three UAVs congregating at a potential target to identify it definitively. In our second simulation, we consider a scenario with a single UAV within an AOI and target distribution identical to the first simulation. This scenario corresponds to a non-swarming centralized model for ATR where target recognition is done at the base station. The relative times for identifying the three targets shown in Table 6(a) illustrate that the swarmed model for ATR performs more efficiently than the centralized model while identifying increasing number of targets in a large AOI.

Figure 6(b) shows the update of anti-pheromone by UAVs in a simulation with mobile targets. As the mobile target changes location, older pheromone values corresponding to previous locations of the potential target get diminished

No. of targets	Time to identify target with swarm	Time to identify target in central-ized model
1	55	11
2	133	519
4	184	Not discovered

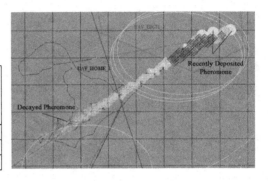

Fig. 6. (a) Comparison of the times required for target identification using a swarmed model vs. using a centralized model for ATR. (b) Snapshot from a COMSTAR simulation illustrating the subtractive pheromone update by different UAVs while tracking a mobile target.

(light colored circles) due to anti-pheromone deposited by a UAV visiting the target that cannot determine the target at that location. Correspondingly, UAVs deposit pheromone (dark colored circles) at the locations recently visited by the mobile target as illustrated by the larger solid dots at the top right corner of Figure 6(b).

6   Related Work

Over the past decade, algorithms inspired by natural adaptive systems such as insect colonies have been applied to various complex problems including the traveling salesman problem (TSP) [1, 6], telecom network routing [5, 11], and distributed information search [3, 4]. In most these systems, the nodes of the network along which ants deposit pheromone are stationary. In contrast, for the COMSTAR system, the nodes of the network reprsented by the UAVs are provided with mobility to search and locate mobile targets. a priori, the targets can be mobile. Multi-agent systems [12] provide a suitable framework for implementing decentralized algorithms through interactions between entities. Software agents are used widely for various commercial and military applications such as Virtual Information Processing Agent Research (VIPAR) and Boeing Inc.'s LogNet. In [10], an insect based swarming algorithm for ATR is described. In contrast to their work, the UAV algorithms described in this paper use deterministic foraging when there are no available potential targets, and, take into account the UAV's current mission and the characteristics of a potential target characteristics before deciding to move towards the potential target.

7   Conclusion and Future Work

In this paper we have described swarming algorithms for ATR using a multi-agent system. The swarmed model addresses problems in the centralized model for ATR such as scalability in the number of UAVs and network congestion and reliability of the central location. Our simulation results show that the swarmed model compares favorably with the centralized model as the number of targets and the size of the AOI increases. This work has been our first step in developing a swarming algorithm for ATR. We are currently improving different features of the COMSTAR system. We are investigating an improved communication protocol based on a decision theoretic mechanism that enables a UAV to identify other suitable UAVs to exchange gossiped information with. Another area we are investigating involves dynamically partitioning the AOI as the swarm operates. Specifically, we are interested in the problem of ensuring consistent coverage of different regions in the AOI to prevent honey pot-like attacks on the system. Finally, we are investigating reliable communication protocols using bayesian updates to address issues related to security and fault tolerance in the system.

Acknowledgements. This work has been supported through DoD NavAir STTR grant no. N00014-04-M-0290.

References

1. E. Bonabeau, M. Dorigo and G. Theraulaz, "Swarm Intelligence: From Natural to Artificial Systems," Oxford University Press, 1999.
2. M. Cohen, "An Introduction to Automatic Target Recognition," EW Design Engineers' Handbook, 1989-1990, pp. 2-1 - 2-2.
3. P. Dasgupta, "Improving Peer-to-Peer Resource Discovery Using Mobile Agent Based Referrals," Lecture Notes in Computer Science, Springer, Vol. 2872, Proc. of AP2PC 2003, pp. 186-197.
4. P. Dasgupta, "Intelligent Agent Enabled Peer-to-Peer Search Using Ant-based Heuristics," Proc. of the Intl. Conf. on Artificial Intelligence, 2004, pp. 351-357.
5. G. Di Caro and M. Dorigo, "AntNet: Distributed Stigmergetic Control for Communications Networks," Journal of AI Research, vol 9, 1998, pp. 317-365.
6. F. Gaudiano, Shargel, and E. Bonabeau, "Control of UAV swarms: What the bugs can teach us" AIAA Unmanned Unlimited, 2003.
7. K. Nordberg, P. Forssen, J. Wiklund, "A flexible runtime system for image processing in a distributed computational environment for an unmanned aerial vehicle," Proceedings of IWSSIP 02, Manchester, UK, 2002.
8. Office of Naval Research, "Image Processing for Automatic Target Recognition,"
9. M. Portmann and A. Seneviratne, "Cost-effective broadcast for fully decentralized peer-to-peer networks," Computer Communication, Special Issue on Ubiquitous Computing, Elsevier Science, Autumn 2002.
10. J. Sauter, R. Matthews, H. Parunak, S. Brueckner, "Performance of Digital Pheromones for Swarming Vehicle Control," AAMAS 2005(accepted).
11. R. Schoonderwood, O Holland, J Bruten, L Rothkrantz, "Ant-based load balancing in Telecommunication Networks," Adaptive Behavior, vol 5, 1996, pp. 169-207.
12. G. Weiss (ed.), "Multiagent Systems: A Modern Approach to Distributed Artificial Intelligence," MIT Press, 1998.

Analysis and Run-Time Verification of Dynamic Security Policies

Helge Janicke, François Siewe, Kevin Jones,
Antonio Cau, and Hussein Zedan

Software Technology Research Laboratory,
Gateway House, De Montfort University,
Leicester LE1 9BH
{heljanic, fsiewe, kij, acau, hzedan}@dmu.ac.uk

Abstract. Ensuring the confidentiality, integrity and availability of information is the key issue in the battle for information superiority and thus is a decisive factor in modern warfare. Security policies and security mechanisms govern the access to information and other resources. Their correct specification, i.e. denial of potentially dangerous access and adherence to all established need-to-know requirements, is critical. In this paper we present a security model that allows to express dynamic access control policies that can change on time or events. A simple agent system, simulating a platoon, is used to show the need and the advantages of our policy model. The paper finally presents how existing tool-support can be used for the analysis and verification of policies.

1   Introduction

Fast and reliable access to information is becoming one of the major factors that decide on the success of a military operation. Modern technologies, such as airborne sensors and satellite imaging, provide more detailed and accurate data about the physical domain than ever before. The amount of information helps to lower uncertainty whilst new technologies to communicate information, help to develop shared situational awareness.

The sheer load of information also has its drawbacks. Commanders that need to make decisions quickly might not have the capability to analyse and comprehend the provided information in time. Decision making processes are therefore supported by systems that are capable of analysing, filtering, combining and presenting information that is relevant to the scenario. Such a system can be seen as a Multi Agent System in which Software Agents represent the information sources and processors that assist in human decision making [1, 2, 3].

The agent system that is providing, processing and communicating the information, together with the information itself, forms the information domain. It is information that is becoming increasingly important with the rise of Network Centric Warfare, and concerns about its availability, confidentiality and integrity are predominant factors that decide on the success of military operations [4]. These security requirements are traditionally expressed in security

S.G. Thompson and R. Ghanea-Hercock (Eds.): DAMAS 2005 , LNAI 3890, pp. 92–103, 2006.

policies. Security policies describe properties that the underlying system must implement to be secure. This is usually ensured by adequate security mechanisms, that enforce the policy on the system. Security policies are an invaluable asset to any organisation, especially, when they are based on a sound model, that can be used for the analysis and proof of properties.

Security policies in general deal with all classes of security requirements. We restrict ourself here to those concerned with access control. Most access control models that are available today [5, 6], are of a relatively static nature and make it difficult to express access control requirements that are dependent on time or the occurance of events. These temporal aspects of access control are becoming more important the more flexible ways of communicating information become. Especially in the military domain the value of tactical information, and therefore its protection requirements, will be highly dependent on time (e.g. time to mission start) and events (e.g. adversary action).

Other work [7, 8] has recognised the need for more expressive security policies, to capture the temporal dimension of access control. Although widely recognised, these models lack compositionality. By compositionality we mean that the overall security policy can be composed out of smaller policies that capture specific requirements and that can be verified individually. The advantage of the access control model that is used in our work is that it does not only allow to express parallel, but also sequential composition, which allows to express changes in the policy dependent on time and events. The security model has a sound foundation in Interval Temporal Logic which has been successfully used for functional and temporal system specifications [9] and is now extended to express security properties [10].

The security model and the tool-support for the analysis is part of SANTA development framework, that is concerned with the development of secure Multi Agent Systems. In this framework agents are controlled by security policies, that express security requirements such as authorisation, delegation and obligation. SANTA is unifying, i.e. it allows to express functional, temporal and security requirements within the same formal framework.

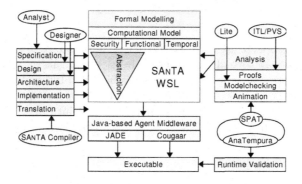

Fig. 1. The SANTA Framework

Beside the sound model, SANTA comprises linguistic support that allows the top-down development of Multi Agent Systems together with their security requirements. The importance of addressing security in the beginning and throughout the development has been widely recognised [11], but there is still a lack of methodology and tool-support. The SANTA framework, depicted in Fig. 1, tries to rectify this situation and draws the focus on security requirements and their interplay with functional and temporal aspects. Starting from a formal specification, the abstract design of the agent system is written in the wide-spectrum language SANTA-WSL, that allows to express abstract specification (as Interval Temporal Logic formulae) and concrete implementation within the same language. SANTA-WSL is close to the popular Java programming language, and contains additional constructs for agent and policy specification. These additions make it easier for an agent-system developer to implement application level security requirements. The SANTA-WSL translator is then used to translate the SANTA-WSL program into an appropriate agent middle-ware. Programs in SANTA-WSL will have a formal semantics and can be analysed using a variety of tools that comprise the SANTA toolkit. This paper will not discuss the development approach itself, but show how access-control policies can be composed to cater for dynamic aspects of security requirements.

Dynamic access control policies are more expressive, but also more difficult to comprehend and analyse. In this paper we will present the prototype of the Security Policy Analysis Tool (SPAT) using a small case study, that illustrates some of the temporal aspects of access-control. The tool will be used to animate the security policy, to show how access control decisions change over time and by events. It allows the analysis of information flow and can provide information on which policy rule is responsible for a concrete access control decision.

The rest of the paper is organised as follows. Section 2 provides a short informal introduction to the underlying logic and the security model. Section 3 then describes a simplified scenario and shows the formalisation of security requirements. Section 4 describes the tool-support for the visualisation and verification of security policies. The final section then concludes and outlines future work.

2   A Dynamic Security Model

This section will provide an overview of how access control requirements can be expressed in our model using small motivating examples. Due to space limitations we do not provide the formal semantics of the model in this paper, but refer the interested reader to [10]. The security model is based on Interval Temporal Logic (ITL), which provides the sound foundation that is necessary in the development of critical systems. We first provide a short informal introduction to ITL, and go then on to introduce our security policies in a small scenario.

2.1   Interval Temporal Logic

Interval Temporal Logic (ITL) is a flexible notation for both propositional and first order reasoning about periods of time found in descriptions of hardware and software systems. It can handle both sequential and parallel composition unlike most temporal logics [12] since assumption/commitment paradigm and a set of compositional guidelines [13] are applied in ITL. There is a very powerful and practical compositional proof system for ITL [12]. That is, much of the proof of a system specified in ITL can be decomposed into proofs of its parts. It offers powerful and extensible specification and proof techniques for reasoning about properties involving safety, liveness and timeliness.

Syntax and Semantics. The key notion of ITL is an *interval*. An interval σ is considered to be a (in)finite sequence of states σ_0, $\sigma_1 \ldots$, where a state σ_i is a mapping from the set of variables Var to the set of values Val. The length $|\sigma|$ of an interval $\sigma_0 \ldots \sigma_n$ is equal to n (one less than the number of states in the interval, i.e., a one state interval has length 0). The syntax of ITL is defined below.

$$\textit{Expressions}$$
$$e ::= \mu \mid a \mid A \mid g(exp_1, \ldots, exp_n) \mid \imath a \colon f$$

$$\textit{Formulae}$$
$$f ::= p(e_1, \ldots, e_n) \mid \neg f \mid f_1 \wedge f_2 \mid \forall v \bullet f \mid \text{skip} \mid f_1 \,;\, f_2 \mid f^*$$

Where μ is an integer value, a is a static variable (doesn't change within an interval), A is a state variable (can change within an interval), v a static or state variable, g is a function symbol and p is a predicate symbol.

The informal semantics of the most interesting constructs are as follows:

- skip: unit interval (length 1, i.e., an interval of two states).
- $f_1 \,;\, f_2$: holds if the interval can be decomposed ("chopped") into a prefix and suffix interval, such that f_1 holds over the prefix and f_2 over the suffix, or if the interval is infinite and f_1 holds for that interval. Note the last state of the interval over which f_1 holds is shared with the interval over which f_2 holds. This is illustrated in Figure 2.
- f^*: holds if the interval is decomposable into a finite number of intervals such that for each of them f holds, or the interval is infinite and can be decomposed into an infinite number of finite intervals for which f holds. Figure 2 illustrates the chopstar operator.

Fig. 2. Chop and Chopstar

Derived Constructs. Following is a list of some derived constructs which are useful for the specification of systems:

- finite $\hat{=} \neg(true\,;false)$: finite interval, i.e., any interval of finite length.
- $\Diamond f \hat{=}$ finite$\,;f$: sometimes f, i.e., any interval such that f holds over a suffix of that interval. Example: $\Diamond X \neq 1 \hat{=}$ finite$\,;X \neq 1$: Any interval such that there exists a state in which X is not equal to 1.
- $\Box f \hat{=} \neg\Diamond\neg f$: always f, i.e., any interval such that f for all suffixes of that interval. Example: $\Box X = 1 \hat{=} \neg($finite$\,;X \neq 1)$: Any interval such that the value of X is equal to 1 in all states of that interval.
- fin $f \hat{=} \Box($empty $\supset f)$: final state, i.e., any interval such that f holds in the final state of that interval.

2.2 Security Policies

Access control policies are expressed in terms of subjects, objects and actions. Subjects represent active entities, such as users and processes, that can be authenticated within the system. We denote the set of all subjects by S. The system state is represented by objects. Objects can only be modified by the execution of actions on request of authenticated subjects. We denote the set of all objects by O, the set of all actions by A. The access control policy determines whether a subject is allowed to perform an action on an object, or not.

In the context of a Multi Agent System, each agent is seen as both, subject and object. As a subject, it is a uniquely identifiable process that acts on behalf of another agent or user. As an object, it encapsulates its state. In our case contains information about the physical domain, such as images, positions or other tactical information, that requires protection.

Traditionally access control policies are defined in terms of rules that capture access control requirements [14]. The general form of a rule is:

$$premise \longrightarrow consequence$$

The premise of a rule determines when the rule *fires* and the consequence of the rule determines the outcome of the rule, for example an access control decision. We follow this approach, but allow the premise of a rule to express a behaviour rather than a predicate. The intuition is that an authorisation can be dependent on the history of execution rather than only the currently observable state. This allows to express history dependent authorisations such as the Chinese Wall Policy [15]. The following example shows such a rule:

$$\left(\begin{array}{l} \forall s \in S, o \in O, a \in A\cdot \\ \Diamond do(s,o,a) \wedge clientinfo(c,o) \wedge \\ sepconcern(c,c') \wedge clientinfo(c',o') \end{array} \right) \mapsto autho^-(s,o',a) \qquad (1)$$

Where the predicates have the following meaning:

- $do(s,o,a)$: Subject s performs action a on object o.
- $clientinfo(c,o)$: Object o belongs to client c.
- $sepconcern(c,c')$: Client c and client c' are in a separation of concern relationship.

The rule given in Eq. 1 then states that when a subject has at some point in time accessed information of a client, the same subject cannot (negative authorisation denoted by $autho^-$) access information about a client that is in a separation of concern relationship.

The informal semantics of operator $\mapsto$ (*Followed By*), that is used in the rules is: Whenever f holds for a subinterval, w holds in the last state of that subinterval. This is depicted in the figure below.

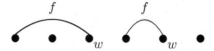

The right-hand side of a rule in the security model contains either the variable $autho$, $autho^+$ or $autho^-$. This allows to express hybrid access control policies, in which both positive authorisation ($autho^+$) and negative authorisation ($autho^-$) can be expressed. In case of conflicts, i.e. a subject has both positive and negative authorisation, a conflict resolution rule ($autho$) determines the actual access decision. Eq. 2 shows a conflict resolution rule, stating that a negative authorisation takes precedence over a positive authorisation.

$$autho^+(S,O,A) \wedge \neg autho^-(S,O,A) \mapsto autho(S,O,A) \qquad (2)$$

We denote universally quantified variables by uppercase letters. Rules form the basis of our access control model. A simple policy can be seen as a set of these rules, where the intuition is that all rules apply simultaneously.

To capture the dynamics of certain security requirements and to allow the incremental development of security policies, policies can be composed using a rich set of operators. The following depicts a selection of operators with their informal semantics.

- $[P\,;Q] \mathrel{\widehat=} [P]\,;[Q]$: Sequential composition of two policies. The system is first governed by policy P and then by policy Q.
- $[P\|Q] \mathrel{\widehat=} [P] \wedge [Q]$: Parallel composition of two policies. The system is governed by policy P and Q at the same time.
- $[\langle w \rangle P] \mathrel{\widehat=} [[\neg w]P]$: The system is governed by policy P unless w holds. The state formula w can here indicate the happening of an event.
- $[[w]P] \mathrel{\widehat=} ([P] \wedge \Box w) \vee ((([P] \wedge \Box w)\,;\mathsf{skip}) \wedge \mathsf{fin}\,\neg w) \vee (\mathsf{empty} \wedge \neg w)$: The system is governed by policy P as long as w holds.

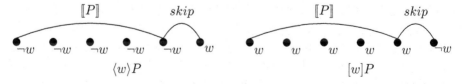

Policy composition can be used for the incremental development of security policies. The advantage of this approach is that small policies are easier to comprehend and verify. The compositional operators can then be used for the integration of the overall system policy. We presented only a selection of operators that are used in the following case-study. The policy model provides a wider range of operators, for example to allow the dynamic addition/ deletion of rules or to select different policies according to the happening of an event or a time-out, whichever is first.

3   Case Study

We present a small simplified scenario, that shows the use of our dynamic policy model. We will use this scenario in the subsequent section, to illustrate the functionality of our analysis toolkit.

Scenario. *A platoon is navigating an area, where long range communication is limited due to environmental conditions. The platoon consists of several small units and a command unit that carries a long distance transmitter. The communication within the platoon is enabled using short distance radio links. The quality of service of the long distance transmission is highly dependent on the environment the platoon is navigating. Dependent on the command units position there may be significant drops in the communication bandwidth or even areas where communication is not possible at all. The command unit is used to analyse and control the mission. It is constantly relaying mission related information back to the base and provides a relay service to the other members of the platoon. The access to the relay service is controlled by a policy with the following requirements.*

1. All members of the platoon are allowed to relay information.
2. If the bandwidth is dropping below 50% then units that have not been involved in combat action within the last 2 time-units are denied to relay information.
3. If the bandwidth drops below 20% only the command unit can relay tactical and strategic information.
4. If the command unit is under attack, the units that are not in its direct proximity are denied to relay messages, regardless of the available bandwidth.

In the following we will formalise the requirements individually as rules and then show how the rules can be composed to reflect the overall requirement specification. We formalise the first requirement as in Eq. 3

$$member(U, platoon) \land command(CMD, platoon) \mapsto autho^+(U, CMD, relay \quad (3)$$

Where *member* represents the membership relation between units and the platoon, and *command* the command unit relation. If U is a member of *platoon* and CMD is the command unit of the *platoon* it follows that U is authorised to *relay* information via the command unit CMD.

Whilst the first requirement uses only static information, such as the membership, the second requirement includes a temporal aspect. This can be formalised, as in Eq. 4.

$$\begin{pmatrix} \mathsf{fin}\,(bandwidth() < 50) \wedge member(U, platoon) \wedge \\ \neg(\mathsf{finite}\,;\,(\Diamond combat(U) \wedge len(2))) \wedge \\ command(CMD, platoon) \end{pmatrix} \mapsto autho^{-}(U, CMD, relay) \quad (4)$$

If the interval cannot be decomposed into a prefix interval and a suffix interval of length 2, in which sometimes $combat(U)$ holds, and if the bandwidth is in the last state of the interval below 50% then the unit is explicitly denied to relay information via the command unit. The informal semantics of this rule is depicted below.

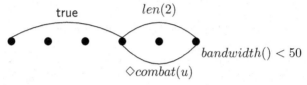

The formalisation of requirement 3 follows the same lines as requirement 2, without the temporal aspect.

$$\begin{pmatrix} bandwidth() < 20 \\ \wedge\, member(U, platoon) \wedge \\ command(CMD, platoon) \end{pmatrix} \mapsto autho^{-}(U, CMD, relay) \quad (5)$$

Requirement 4 finally defines, that if the command unit is under attack, units that are not in its proximity are denied to relay information, regardless of the bandwidth requirements stated in requirements 2 and 3.

$$\begin{pmatrix} combat(CMD) \wedge \\ command(CMD, platoon) \wedge \\ \neg near(CMD, U) \end{pmatrix} \mapsto autho^{-}(U, CMD, relay) \quad (6)$$

The rule in Eq. 6 expresses the requirement. Additionally it states that the rule overrides the requirements 2 and 3. This can be seen as a dynamic change in the security policy, dependent on the event that the command unit is engaged in combat.

The whole policy is expressed as a hybrid policy in which denials take precedence over allowances (Eq. 2). Policy rule 3 holds independently of policy changes. This means in general all members of the platoon have the authorisation to relay information. We distinguish now between two cases:

a) The command unit is not engaged in combat.
b) The command unit is engaged in combat.

The policy for case a) consists of rules 4 and 5, stating that access is limited according to the available bandwidth. It is applied *unless* the command unit is engaged in combat. On this event the policy changes (sequential composition, ;) to case b) defined by rule 6, stating that units in the proximity can relay information. Case b) is applied as long as the command unit is under attack, and is then followed by case a). The composed policy is given in Eq. 7.

$$\{Eq.\,2, Eq.\,3\}\|(\langle combat(CMD)\rangle\{Eq.\,4, Eq.\,5\}\,;\,[combat(CMD)]\{Eq.\,6\})^{*} \quad (7)$$

The advantage of this approach is that access requirements that are dependent on time and events, can be expressed at a higher abstraction level, without the need to explicitly encode the conditions in the premise of the rule. This leads to rules and policies that are easier to comprehend. Using policy composition, the security administrator can then decide on the time and event relations between different policies.

The case-study demonstrates the use of dynamically changing policies, and does show how requirements to control access to resources are specified in general. The model allows to express more traditional security concepts like multi-level security and role-based access control, via the introduction of appropriate predicates. Its compositionality then allows to combine different policies and to reason about properties of the composition.

The semantic model of the security policies allows the formal analysis of the security specification and can be used to prove properties about the specification. In the following we will show how these security policies can be expressed in Tempura, an executable subset of ITL and present tool-support, that assists in the analysis of the given security policy.

4   Analysis and Run-Time Verification

An important reason of choosing ITL is the availability of an executable subset of the logic, known as Tempura [16]. A formula is executable if *i.* it is deterministic, *ii.* the length of the corresponding interval is known and *iii.* the values of the variables (of the formula) are known throughout the corresponding interval. The Tempura interpreter takes a Tempura formula and constructs the corresponding sequence of states, i.e., interval. For more technical details of the interpreter, we refer the reader to [16] which is available from the ITL home-page [17]. The use of ITL, together with its subset of Tempura, offers the benefits of traditional proof methods balanced with the speed and convenience of computer-based testing through execution and simulation. The entire process can remain in one powerful logical and compositional framework.

4.1   Expressing Access Control Policies in Tempura

Executable Temporal Logics have been used for the high-level specification of Multi Agent Systems for a considerable time [18]. Advantages of Tempura are that both parallel and sequential composition is expressible, and that it can closely resemble well known programming language constructs. Tempura has been previously applied to hardware verification and the analysis of time-critical systems [9].

This allows us to model the behaviour of the agent system at a high level and shows how the security policy controls the access to system resources. An access control rule can be expressed in Tempura as follows:

```
define rule1(AuthoP) = { keep {
  forall s < noSubjects :
    forall o < noObjects :
      (member(s,platoon) and command(o,platoon)) implies AuthoP(s,o,relay)=true
}}.
```

Where the predicates **member**, **command** model the relations-ships as in Eq.3. The rules can then be combined using parallel and or sequential composition. The complete policy is shown in the listing below.

```
define policy(AuthoP, AuthoN, Autho) = {
  rule1(AuthoP) and denialtakesprecedence(AuthoP, AuthoN, Autho) and
  ( (halt(combat(cmd)) and rule3(AuthoN) and rule4(AuthoN)) ;
    (halt(not combat(cmd)) and rule5(AuthoN)))
}.
```

The Tempura program representing the system simulation and the policy description is then executed by the Tempura interpreter. The code emits information about current access-control decision in each step of the execution to the graphical analysis tool.

4.2   SPAT

The Security Policy Analysis Tool (SPAT) is used to analyse the behaviour of dynamically changing policies. The graphical front-end can display the access control matrix for all states in the simulation, and it provides interactive filtering mechanisms that make it easier to obtain the required information. Access control information can be displayed in form of an access control matrix, in form of access control lists, or capabilities. The tool also supports the visualisation of delegation and access control decisions, which are not demonstrated in the presented scenario.

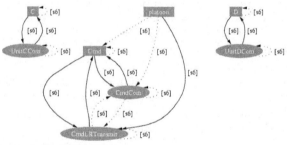

Information Flow Transitive Closure

Especially interesting is the analysis of permissible information flow. By permissible information flow we mean such flows that are allowed by the access control policy. This is a valuable aid in debugging the policy, because a) unwanted information flows can easily be detected and b) restrictions in the policy that violate any *need-to-know* requirements can easily be seen. The figure above depicts the permissible information flow in state 6 of the simulation.

The prototype, that is currently under development, can provide an explanation which rules caused an authorisation or denial. This allows to trace back the rule that lead to an unwanted authorisation and helps in the design of security policies, that match the informal requirement. The figure below depicts the scenario simulation and shows an example explanation.

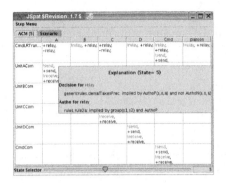
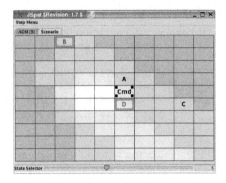

The access control matrix (left picture), together with the explanation component and the graphical visualisation are generic components, that can be used for the analysis of arbitrary security policies. The scenario representation (right picture) is dependent on the scenario itself, but SPAT provides mechanisms for the development of such components and their integration.

5   Conclusion and Future Work

We illustrated the need for dynamically changing security policies using a small military scenario. We presented the security model that underlies the SANTA framework and showed how security policies can be incrementally developed. Unlike most other models, our model allows capturing temporal aspects in both, the premise of authorisation rules and through policy composition. The Security Policy Analysis Tool can then be used to animate and visualise the developed policies, to ensure that the formalisation captured the initial requirements. The tool is especially useful for the analysis of permissible information flow. It allows to write the access control policy tight enough to prohibit malicious behaviour and still ensure that all *need to know* requirements are fullfilled.

Future work will concentrate on the enhancement of the tool support for both the analysis and the linguistic support. In the analysis part we enhance the tracability of access control decisions and increase functionality to filter the visualised information. We also plan to enhance the Tempura interpreter, to allow the animation of a wider class of security policies together with the agent system specification. In the linguistic part we develop the wide-spectrum language SANTA-WSL in which both security and functional aspect can be expressed in a uniform, accessible language at all levels of abstraction.

References

1. Thomas E. Potok, A.S.L., Phillips, L., Pollock, R.: Suitability of agent technology or military command and control in the future combat system environment. In: Proceeding 8th ICCRTS, National Defence University. (2003)
2. Sheldon, F., Potok, T., Kavi, K.: Multi-agent system case studies in command and control, information fusion and data management. In: Journal of Informatica. Volume 28., Solvene Society Informatica (2004) pp 78–89

3. Bharadwajgc, R.: Secure middleware for situation-aware naval c2 and combat systems. In: In Proceedings 9th International Workshop on Future Trends of Distributed Comput ing Systems (FTDCS 2003). (2003)
4. Alberts, D.S.: Understanding information age warfare. CCRP publication series, DoD, US (2001)
5. Jajodia, S., Samarati, P., Subrahmanian, V.S., Bertino, E.: A unified framework for enforcing multiple access control policies. ACM transaction on Database Systems **26** (2001) 214–260
6. Abadi, M., Burrows, M., Lampson, B., Plotkin, G.: A calculus for access control in distributed systems. ACM Transactions on Programming Languages and Systems **15** (1993) 1–29
7. Barker, S., Stuckey, P.J.: Flexible access control specification with constraint logic programming. ACM Transactions on Information & System Security **6** (2003)
8. Bertino, E., Bonatti, P.A., Ferrari, E.: Trbac: A temporal role-based access control model. ACM Trans. Inf. Syst. Secur. **4** (2001) 191–233
9. Cau, A., Czarnecki, C., Zedan, H.: Designing a provably correct robot control system using a lean formal method. In: Proceedings of FTRTFT'98, LNCS 1486. (1998) pp 123–132
10. Siewe, F., Cau, A., Zedan, H.: A compositional framework for access control policies enforcement. In: Proceedings of the ACM workshop on Formal Methods in Security Engineering: From Specifications to Code. (2003)
11. Eckert, C.: Matching security to application needs. In: IFIP TC11 11th International Conference on Information Security. (1995) 237–254
12. Moszkowski, B.: Some very compositional temporal properties. In Olderog, E.R., ed.: Programming Concepts, Methods and Calculi. Volume A-56 of IFIP Transactions., IFIP, Elsevier Science B.V. (North–Holland) (1994) 307–326
13. Zedan, H., Cau, A., Zhou, S.: A calculus for evolution. In: Proc. of The Fifth International Conference on Computer Science and Informatics (CS&I'2000).
14. Woo, T.Y.C., Lam, S.S.: Authorization in distributed systems: A formal approach. In: Proceedings of the 13th IEEE Symposium on Research in security and Privacy, Oakland, California, May 4-6 (1992) 33–50
15. Brewer, D., Nash, M.: The Chinese Wall Policy. In: IEEE Symposium on Research in Security and Privacy. (1989) 206–214
16. Moszkowski, B.: Executing Temporal Logic Programs. Cambridge University Press, England (1986)
17. Cau, A., Moszkowski, B., Zedan, H.:   The ITL homepage.   `http://www.cse.dmu.ac.uk/~cau/itlhomepage/index.html` (2005)
18. Fisher, M.: A survey of concurrent METATEM – the language and its applications. In Gabbay, D.M., Ohlbach, H.J., eds.: Temporal Logic - Proceedings of the First Intemational Conference (LNAI Volume 827), Springer-Verlag: Heidelberg, Germany (1994) 480–505

Cognitive Agents for Sense and Respond Logistics

Kshanti Greene[1], David G. Cooper[1], Anna L. Buczak[2,*],
Michael Czajkowski[1], Jeffrey L. Vagle[1], and Martin O. Hofmann[1]

[1] Lockheed Martin Advanced Technology Laboratories,
3 Executive Campus, 6th Floor,
Cherry Hill, NJ 08002
[2] Sarnoff Corporation, 201 Washington Ave,
Princeton, NJ 08543-5300

Abstract. We present a novel cognitive agent architecture and demonstrate its effectiveness in the Sense and Respond Logistics (SRL) domain. SRL transforms the static, hierarchical architectures of traditional military models into re-configurable networks designed to encourage coordination among small peer units. Multi-agent systems are ideal for SRL because they can provide valuable automation and decision support from low-level control to high-level information synchronization. In particular, agents can be aware of and adapt to changes in the environment that may affect control and decision making. Our architecture, the Engine for Composable Logical Agents with Intuitive Reorganization (ECLAIR) is a framework for enabling rapid development of coherent agent systems that adapt to their environment once deployed. ECLAIR is based on cognitive theories for motivation and adaptation, including Piaget's *Assimilation* and *Accommodation* [21] and Damasio's Somatic Marker Hypothesis [6]. To demonstrate our preliminary work, we implemented a simple simulation environment where our agents handle the ordering and delivery of supplies among operational and supply units in several scenarios requiring adaptation of default behavior.

1 Introduction

Nation states no longer maintain a monopoly on armed forces. This has caused the long-held views of fair conflict to disintegrate, and has fostered the transition to the next stage in the evolution of conflict: fourth generation warfare (4GW) [8]. The technologies developed to aid the warfighter in 4GW must be designed to support dynamic, adaptive operations. Sense and Respond Logistics (SRL) aims to provide precise, agile delivery of supplies to warfighters in these emerging environments [24].

Quick, adaptive response requires small units at the sub-battalion levels of the military hierarchy to be both more autonomous in their control, and more coordinated in their actions. Multi-agent systems can represent the varied roles of specific units and assets involved in logistics. They can automate some behaviors such as ordering supplies and prioritizing requests, and they can build an awareness of the world and other agents that

---

* Work done while at LM ATL.

S.G. Thompson and R. Ghanea-Hercock (Eds.): DAMAS 2005 , LNAI 3890, pp. 104–120, 2006.

allows them to enhance the decision making of unit commanders. Most importantly, automated behaviors and decision support must be adaptive to changes in the environment, and often behaviors and decisions must be coordinated with other units or agents.

We have developed a cognitive agent architecture that builds a framework for adaptive control and coordinated decision support. This paper discusses preliminary results using the architecture in the SRL domain. The Engine for Composable Logical Agents with Intuitive Reorganization (ECLAIR) incorporates the main mechanisms from Piaget's Cognitive-Stage Theory of Development [21], and it uses concepts from Damasio's Somatic Marker Hypothesis [6] to discover what should be learned. ECLAIR agents contain modules for stimuli, awareness, plan behavior, reflex behavior, control/decision making, and adaptivity. The interaction between awareness, behavior and adaptivity allows agents to modify their behavior based on their perception of world and self states. Self states are represented by homeostatic vectors (HVs), in which the comfortable level is a range, not a threshold. Agent wellbeing is an emotional state that is computed as a function of the agent's homeostatic vectors.

In normal situations, ECLAIR agents act logically, using plans, or workflows, when there is a known strategy to accomplish a task. However, when quick reaction is needed, motivation for action is intuitive or reflexive. In traditional logistic systems, plans for action were pre-defined and static [24]. In normal operation, a pre-set plan may be suitable as it gives agents a guide for consistent behavior. However, in SRL, "normal" operation is often interrupted by events such as the appearance of a new adversary. In these cases, the need for dynamic re-planning is clear, and is provided in our agent architecture. Yet sometimes, even generating a new plan can be too time consuming for immediate survival. In these cases, our agents use adaptive, reflexive behavior that allows them to respond faster to unexpected or drastic changes in the environment, such as a loss of a supply unit when an engaged unit is dangerously low on ammunition. If an agent's perception of wellbeing indicates an urgent situation, reflexes will be fired in order to elicit immediate attention.

Adaptivity in ECLAIR effects both logical (cognitive) and reflexive behaviors. Cognitive adaptivity involves learning parameter and structure modifications for improved agent workflows using a genetic programming approach that was discussed in previous work [2]. Reflexive behaviors are adjusted to adapt to dynamic changes in the environment using a technique based on reinforcement learning [15, 27, 26] that we describe later. ECLAIR was developed as an extension to the Extensible Mobile Agent Architecture (EMAA) that has been applied to many military applications [2]. EMAA deals with agent communication accross various networks, while ECLAIR extends agent behavior. We demonstrate ECLAIR's cognitive architecture and reflexive adaptation using a simplistic simulation of net-centric warfare logistics and show that agents are able to adapt their reflexive behavior to compensate for unexpected events in the environment.

This paper is organized as follows. Section 2 discusses related work in agents in military applications and logistics. Section 3 introduces Sense and Respond Logistics and describes its background, requirements, and challenges. Section 3 also discusses why agents represent SRL well, and what is required by the agent system to be effective for SRL. Section 4 describes our agent architecture and details our approach to plan and reflex adaptivity. Section 5 describes our logistics application and shows the results that indicate that agent adaptivity improves speed of command. We conclude with future work in Section 6 and concluding remarks in Section 7.

2 Related Work

2.1 Agents in Military and Logistics Applications

Adaptive agents is a well-studied topic that spans many approaches and domains [18, 7, 11]. Other agent systems exist that simulate the military domain and deal with the problems in it, but none of these systems approach the domain with the modern view of Net-Centric Warfare and Sense and Respond Logistics. TacAir-SOAR [14] is an expert system-based agent application for automated flight control and battlefield simulation developed using the rule-based, cognitive system SOAR. This system may be well-suited to the previous military application models that had completely predefined knowledge and problem models, but would not adapt well to 4GW. In today's battlefield environments, the environment and the adversarial agents in it cannot be completely modeled and any existing rules must be adaptive to environment changes. Unfortunately, sophisticated as it is, TacAir-SOAR has become obsolete for modern battlefields because it is not flexible.

Another agent system for battlefield simulation is the University XXI project [13]. This system begins to tackle cooperation among units, but it deals with larger units at the battalion level, not small, mobile units. A transition in military thought is occurring that believes that the difficulty is in controlling lower level units, while control at a higher level (tactical strategy) is both more understood and more able to be controlled by human commanders [24]. This system also uses the rules pre-built into it for all behaviors. Although it is reactive, it is not adaptive.

An advanced logistics program was initiated in 1996 [25] to explore logistics planning and execution during Operations Desert Shield and Desert Storm. It was theorized that if information systems had better been able to handle specific logistics problems such as scheduling and coordination, then significant improvements would have been possible in resource sequencing and overall control over the supply chain. Thus, the challenge for ALP was to develop the technology to support an end-to-end logistics system with automated plan generation, execution monitoring, end-to-end movement control, and rapid supply and sustainment. To address this challenge the ALP team developed the ALP agent architecture. This architecture provided advanced research into the areas of cognitive agency, fine-grained information management and component-based design. Core pieces of the ALP architecture were made publicly available as open source as the COGnitive Agent ARchitecture (COUGAAR) [12].

Lockheed Martin Advanced Technology Laboratories (LM ATL) has developed agent technology that offers promising solutions to the problems underlined in SRL. LM ATL has applied agent technology in several projects covering a full range of intelligent systems, including information management for time-sensitive strike, situation awareness for small military units, execution of user requests entered via spoken language, and human aiding tools for the Navy Fleet Battle Experiments [4, 5, 9, 19, 10, 20]. ECLAIR extends our previous work and bridges concepts developed for ALP and COUGAAR with research in cognitive and adaptive agents.

2.2 Cognitive Architectures

The two leading cognitive architectures with a psychological basis are SOAR [17] and ACT-R [1]. Both are hypotheses for answering Allen Newell's concept of a Unified Theory of Cognition [23]. Newell saw that in a person, there are many interacting components that must be integrated into a single comprehensive system, and believed that the single system is the source of all behavior. Thus, the goal of a cognitive architecture is to have one system that represents the behavior of the many components that make up a thinking person. ACT-R and SOAR were developed based on contemporary psychological experimental results, and were not built on specific developmental theories.

ACT-R is a cognitive architecture designed as an integration of components discovered in psychology research [1]. This model is primarily meant to accurately simulate human behavior. Given a specific cognitive theory, ACT-R can be used to model the components of the theory. Once the model has been created, experiments can be made in order to get results very similar to human experimental results. In addition, the model can be used to extend previous theories by creating a novel experiment for the model. ACT-R also has a set of modules that represent different functional aspects of the brain. The interaction between these modules happens by each module exposing part of its activity into a buffer. The central production system uses the data in the buffers for its processing. ACT-R has primarily been used for psychological research, but has also been used to simulate computer generated forces for training purposes.

SOAR is a cognitive architecture focused on the functional requirements of human level intelligence. The three constraints that SOAR attempts to satisfy are goal driven behavior, continuous learning from experience, and showing "real time cognition." The goal is to have a system where memory can be directly used for action. A production system is at the heart of the architecture. The decision cycle has seven steps: Input, State Elaboration, Propose Operator, Compare Operators, Select Operator, Apply Operator, and Output [22]. SOAR's mechanism for learning, called "chunking," has proven to cause unexpected results, and in many systems, such as TacAir-SOAR, has been turned off. Recently, experiments have been done to add reinforcement learning techniques to SOAR in place of the "chunking" mechanism [22]. While developing the ECLAIR architecture, ACT-R and SOAR were considered as possible starting points, but both were found to have a different approach that did not consider adaptivity as the basis for developing a cognitive architecture.

3 Motivation

3.1 Sense and Respond Logistics

Net-Centric Warfare (NCW) addresses the capabilities for 4GW and aims to combine "information-age concepts in the evolving strategic environment, enabling dispersed, semi-autonomous combat capability packages that produce coherent, mass effects via speed and coordinated efforts" [24]. Sense and Respond Logistics (SRL), is the process that handles the supply chain in 4GW. In NCW, sustaining operating tempo (OPTEMPO) is as much a logistics issue as it is kinetic. In order to maintain appropriate warfighting capability levels, the supply chain must not be interrupted. Unplanned operational pauses due to logistics problems are considered planning and adaptability failures. As the battlespace becomes ever more complex, the need for agile, robust logistics support of warfighter maneuvering becomes more crucial. As a result, current logistics planning is quickly becoming obsolete. Increasing numbers of asynchronous threats and specialized missions have caused the logistics problem to evolve. SRL must also operate in an uncertain environment in which actions that have a positive effect today may not have the same results tomorrow.

An ideal situation for logistics is that all troops are supplied with the right goods at the right time, however, hierarchical distribution systems have had little success in scenarios requiring just-in-time (JIT) delivery. One solution to this problem consists of bringing decision making for changing supply routes and determining priorities down to the squad and unit level. This allows the system to be more adaptive since small units can react to changes without restructuring the global mission. However, the optimization of logistics tasks in a sub-battalion NCW environment is an optimization problem with a moving target, a.k.a. a dynamic optimization problem. Machine learning has proven to be a good tool to deal with such a moving target. Our system uses machine learning techniques to allow for adaptivity, particularly at the sub-battalion levels of the command tree.

3.2   Agent Systems for SRL

According to the United States Department of Defense [24], a networked, heterogeneous multi-agent system is needed to support Sense and Respond Logistics. These agents should represent all roles in the logistics domain, including the operational units (consumers), suppliers, and assets. In our agent architecture, roles are developed by supplying default stimuli and motivation to initiate action, and plans and reflexes to handle action. We are able to completely separate the agent architecture from the domain-specific extension. Methodologies for defining the initial agent behavior using XML and extended key classes from the ECLAIR architecture are provided for the agent developer.

Automated aides are another SRL system requirement to support cognitive decision making [24]. These aids can take the form of automated control by the agent or agent-assisted decision support for the warfighters. In this paper we discuss methods, based on a cognitive agent architecture, to provide automation for low-level control normally handled by humans. This frees warfighters to concentrate on more complex aspects of warfare. Our command and control is in the form of tasks for an agent. A task is a unit of action, for example, an action to move or to make a request. A plan or workflow is a series of tasks, and a reflex is a single task.

The other aspect of decision support involves supplying a user with information and options in the form of a recommender system. This will aid the user with decisions that still need to be made by a human. The recommender system can be an extension of the automated agent control system. An agent will use the same decision process to find the best plan of action, but instead of completing the task autonomously, it will supply weighted options to the user and complete the task based on the user's input. We will be focusing on this capability in our future work.

4   The ECLAIR Agent Architecture for Adaptivity

4.1   The ECLAIR Process Loop

Theoretical Background. ECLAIR is a cognitive model based on developmental cognitive psychology research and neuropsychological research. Though many developmental theories contributed to the ECLAIR model, the two most prominent in the architecture are Piaget's adaptation theory [21], and Damasio's Somatic Marker Hypothesis [6]. Piaget's adaptation theory consists of three main concepts: *Assimilation, Accommodation,* and *Equilibration. Assimilation* processes unfamiliar input in the same way that one would process the most similar, familiar input. *Accommodation* changes the processes to deal with unfamiliar input. Finally, *Equilibration,* balances the aforementioned processes.

The *Somatic Marker Hypothesis* stems from Damasio's belief that reasoning is not the only basis for decisions, but that decisions can also originate from gut feelings. A somatic marker is defined by Damasio as a trigger that recalls feelings related to the available decisions. The decision is made based on the best expected feeling given the available actions for the current circumstance. Each memory of feelings becomes a somatic marker that is used as a map from circumstance to action.

Our cognitive model approaches the processing problem from the perspective of interaction with the environment. This is similar to the Observation, Orientation, De-

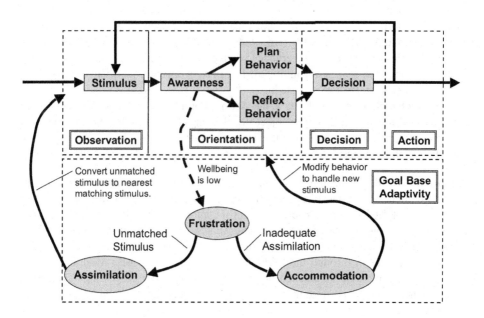

Fig. 1. The ECLAIR Process Loop. The Goal-Based Adaptivity loop listens to the decision loop during processing. When the agent wellbeing goes down, the agent becomes frustrated and determines the source of frustration. Once the source is determined, either Assimilation or Accomodation processing is enacted to adapt to the frustration.

cision, and Action (OODA) loop model used in military operations [28]. We extend
the OODA loop model with a clear representation for learning and development. Our
model contains two interdependent processes. The first is the decision loop that closely
reflects the OODA loop, and the second is the adaptivity loop that observes the decision
loop until adaptation is needed (Figure 1).

Perception. Instead of Observation, a cognitive model has *perception*. Perception affects both external and internal features. For a living being, external perception is in the
form of sensed sound, smell, sight, taste, and touch, while internal perception includes
hunger, pain, and comfort. ECLAIR's Stimulus and Awareness Modules interact within
an agent to create stimuli from external and internal perceptions. Orientation for a cognitive model occurs through interaction between perception, attention, and memory.
Orientation links the agent's model of self and the world with its available behaviors
and creates the basis for decision making.

In ECLAIR, when the Awareness module receives a stimulus, it matches the stimulus
with reflex and plan behaviors that have the stimulus type as a condition. Stimuli may
also update the agent's self and world representations. Self representations are in the
form of Homeostatic Vectors (HVs), indicating ideal values for various aspects of the
agent, such as hunger or tiredness. HVs are based on Damasio's somatic markers and
are a mechanism for having multiple goal states. Wellbeing, or the 'state of mind' of an
agent is an aggregate of the homeostatic variables.

Action. Damasio's Somatic Marker Hypothesis expands theories of the nature of decision making to include reactive behavior in addition to reasoning. ECLAIR combines
the decision making behavior of two methods in order to decide on an action. Behavior
is either handled by a reflex by adherence to a plan. If a reflex is fired, the activity within
it will be completed if it is not inhibited. If a plan is enacted, the plan will continue
unless a higher priority plan is started.

In the OODA loop, the final step is the Action. For a human, examples of action are
speaking, moving, manipulating an object and glancing. Agents on the other hand may be
sending data, retrieving data, computing, sending control commands, ordering supplies,
etc. The action is encapsulated in an activity chosen during the decision making stage.

Adaptivity. We define adaptivity as the ability to modify agent functionality to suit
the environment or internal state. Learning is a mechanism that helps develop an agents
ability to adapt. ECLAIR's Goal-Based Adaptivity module can modify and extend functionality at any stage of the OODA loop. The Adaptivity Module listens to events from
all other modules that are relevant for learning.

As input comes in through the Stimulus Module, the Awareness Module matches
what it can and puts the unmatched input in a queue for later processing. The queue
of unmatched input is one starting point for adaptivity through *Assimilation*. As performance decreases, the HVs will move away from their ideal levels, causing low wellbeing. This will trigger adaptivity to find a better action using *Accomodation*.

During the *Assimilation* phase, the agent adapts its orientation. Rather than setting
aside the input, the agent translates the input into a form that can be processed. During
the *Accommodation* phase, the agent creates a modified action for the input. This requires

small changes to: orientation, since the inputs have to be distinguished; decision, since a new input condition has to be matched to a behavior; and action, since a new action or set of actions may be required to successfully accommodate to the novel input. Successful accommodation will be recognized by the agent through improved wellbeing.

In the first iteration of ECLAIR we focused on adaptation in the *Accommodation* category, as agents modify their behaviors to suit their environment. The structure of the Goal-Based Adaptivity Module allows for different learning mechanisms to be used. The plan adaptivity and reflex adaptivity methods described below are examples of two such learning mechanisms. Our plan adaptivity scheme is based on genetic programming. A reinforcement learning based approach was implemented in ECLAIR for reflex adaptivity. More details of the ECLAIR architecture are available in [3].

4.2 Plan Adaptivity

An ECLAIR agent's plan, also called a workflow, is a list of tasks linked by execution paths that can be conditional or unconditional. Tasks on an unconditional path are always executed, while tasks on a conditional path are executed only if the condition is met. Each task can take a certain number of task dependant parameters. The plan adaptivity mechanism was designed for this type of workflow.

Our approach to plan adaptivity is named Evolutionary Platform for Agent Learning (EPAL) and was described in detail in [2]. Genetic programming (GP) invented by John Koza [16] constitutes the basis for adaptivity in EPAL. GP uses the principles of Darwinian evolution for performing program synthesis by genetically breeding a population of computer programs. The basic operators of reproduction, crossover and mutation operate on individuals in the population and a fitness function describes how good a given individual is. In GP each individual program is represented as a tree.

In EPAL we represent agent plans in a GP tree form and GP operators work on agents' genetic material (i.e., GP trees) to generate new agents that have learned to overcome certain problems in their environment. EPAL's main GP building blocks are the individual tasks that compose a workflow. As agents execute in the environment their fitness is collected. The value of fitness guides the evolutionary learning process. The method developed is a general method that can generate completely new agent plans, as well as related plans but with new parameters. Augmenting an agent's plan is synonymous with changing the agent's behavior, thus the method can be used for generating new behaviors as well.

We have not used the EPAL agent adaptivity in a logistics scenario yet, although we are currently integrating EPAL into ECLAIR's plan and adaptivity modules. We have demonstrated EPAL's operation and usefulness in a scenario similar to Fleet Battle Experiment-Juliet (FBE-J). Our experiment showed that agents learned to match sending rates of messages with the urgency of the messages to generate plans that improve overall network performance [2].

4.3 Reflex Adaptivity

A reflex in ECLAIR is composed of a stimulus, an activity, and a set of parameters for the activity (Figure 2). We use an approach based on reinforcement learning (RL)

[15, 27] to learn the best parameters to use in an activity given the stimulus. Reinforcement learning is based on two major principles; receiving immediate reinforcement for taking an action given the state of the environment, and generating an overall value for a state-action mapping using delayed reward. Our reinforcement problem calculates the overall value of stimulus-activity-parameter mappings from the reward received as the results of activities are observed. The innovation in our technique is not in the technical aspects of our RL algorithm, but in integrating cognitive elements from the architecture, such as perception and expectation. We focus on these aspects of the algorithm.

Fig. 2. A reflex in ECLAIR. Contains a stimulus, activity, and parameters to the activity.

A typical reinforcement learning problem is composed of a set of discrete states, S, and a set of discrete actions, A. The high-level goal is to learn the best mapping between state and action ($s \rightarrow a$, $s \in S$, $a \in A$), or the best *policy*. In our architecture, a state is composed of a stimulus and an activity. Stimuli in our logistics scenarios include internal states (represented as HVs) such as LOW_FUEL and VERY_LOW_FOOD. Given these internal states, our agents will take an action; for example, ORDER_FUEL and ORDER_FOOD, respectively. We create S from combinations of stimuli and activities. In our current logistics application, S is pre-defined, however, *Accommodation* could be used to extend S.

The parameters to the activity, for example who to order from, how much to order, and what priority the order should be, are variable and constitute our learning problem. We create A from the occurring combinations of parameters: $A = \bigcup_{i=1}^{m} \Phi_i, \Phi_i = P_1 \times P_2 \cdots \times \cdots P_j \cdots \times \cdots P_n$, where P_j is a parameter type and all its values, n is the number of parameter types for activity i, and m is the number of activities. Our policies are then composed of {stimulus-activity}-{parameter set} mappings, corresponding to RL's state-action ($s \rightarrow a$) mappings: $s = \{\sigma, \lambda\}$, $a = \phi$, where $\sigma \in \Sigma$, $\lambda \in \Lambda$, and $\phi \in \Phi_i$. Our adaptivity module for reflex behavior stores overall values for policies that it computes over time.

Reinforcement is computed by comparing the expectation of the activity with the observations that are seen as a result of the activity occurring. This was the main challenge in our approach as the observations from an activity are not immediate and may not be seen until several intermediate tasks are completed. For example, in our logistics simulation, the expectation from ORDER_FUEL is that we will receive the amount of FUEL we ordered *within a certain period of time*. In order for an agent to receive a resource, a supplying agent must receive the order for the resource, and then must send out an asset to complete the order, assuming it has the asset and resource available. The whole operation could potentially take several simulated days, even with a relatively fast chain of command. If the supplying agent does not have an available asset or the requested resource, the order may never be filled.

Reinforcement is based on a value, XVO that is computed as follows. When an agent fires a reflex, its awareness module generates an *expectation* object that indicates the expected results, as well as a time that the result should be expected by. When the agent receives a stimulus, it generates an *observation* object if the stimulus is of a type in which it is interested. The agent then attempts to match the *observation* with an *expectation* using a map function indicating which reflexes cause which observations. For example, a RECEIVED_FUEL observation may have occurred because of an OR-DER_FUEL reflex. If a match occurs between the *observation* and an *expectation*, the agent's adaptivity module then compares the details of the *expectation* with the *observation* to generate an *expectation* versus *observation* (XVO) value. The XVO value is between -1.0 (does not meet expectations) and 1.0 (meets expectations). If the *observation* does not occur within an extended period of time, an *expired observation* will be created, and XVO will be -1.0. If the *observation* occurred within the expected time, and had the correct parameters, then the XVO will be 1.0. Values between -1.0 and 1.0 could occur if the *observation* was late, or had only part of the requested resources. Like motivation and behavior, the expectation object is configurable, so various methods for computing XVO could be used. Figure 3 shows the process flow for reflexes.

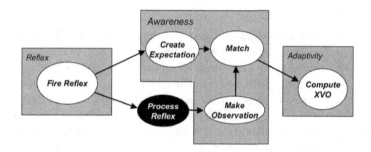

Fig. 3. The process flow for a reflex in ECLAIR. The white nodes show the behavior of the agent firing the reflex. Gray boxes represent the modules that handle the nodes. The black node could be handled by other agents.

Reinforcement value is a function of the XVO and the change in homeostatic vectors that may occur due to a reflex being fired. This causes the awareness module to consider that even if the reflex yielded the expected results, it may not have been the correct approach if it did not improve our situation. Reinforcement is given to the policy that caused the *observation* to occur, as well as previous policies that have been attempted that used common parameters in the same situation. We are attempting to generalize reinforcement without over-fitting (reinforcing the wrong behavior).

Formally, the reinforcement, r, for any policy that has been used while running the system is:

$$r = \gamma^{-i}\alpha(XVO + \Delta HV)\frac{|P_p \cap P_o|^{\sigma}}{|P_p|}$$

Where $i \equiv$ the age of the policy being rewarded (most recent=1), $\Delta HV =$ the change in homeostatic vector level (positive= improved, negative=deteriorated), $P_p =$ the set of parameters in the policy's activity, P_o = the set of parameters in the observation, and γ, α and σ are learning-rate variables.

Overall value for a policy is the summation of its reinforcement, r, over time. When selecting a policy to use for a given state, usually the policy with the highest overall value is used. However, exploration will occur at a rate dependent on the wellbeing of the agent. The rate is a value in $[0 \cdots 1]$ indicating the percentage of time a random change in the action should be made. If wellbeing is high, then the agent has a good set of behaviors and will decrease the exploration rate. However, if wellbeing is low, then the agent will increase the rate so that it will explore more often and perhaps discover behaviors that will improve wellbeing. Exploration is a key component of reinforcement learning as it allows the agent interacting with the system to try actions that it may not have tried if it was only considering the current "best" action [27]. Our solution elegantly incorporates knowledge about our internal state to compute an exploration rate that is well suited to the cognitive architecture.

5   Application

5.1   Logistics Simulation

We developed a demonstration application that shows how ECLAIR agent adaptivity applies to logistics. The prototype shows preliminary solutions to two important SRL goals. ECLAIR agents improve the speed of command in a robust fashion and adapt to the changes in a demand driven network. The scenarios we describe do not attempt to show the full application of Sense and Respond Logistics, however they do demonstrate the agent architecture's ability to react appropriately in a dynamic environment. We also have not compare results with other field-tested logistics applications, so the hypothesis that adaptive agents improves performance in a real-world environment is yet to be affirmed.

Figure 4 depicts the application's interface. ECLAIR agents represent three operational units (OU) (boxes with an X) and two supply units (SU) (boxes with a horizontal line). As an OU, the ECLAIR agent monitors its homeostatic states that indicate how much fuel, ammunition, and food it has. As the OU consumes its resources, it becomes increasingly unhappy until it is stimulated to request a re-supply. Re-supply requests are drawn as arrow-headed lines pointing to the SU the request was sent to. OUs set their expectations based on how much of a resource they requested and how long they expect to wait for the request to be fulfilled. When supplied, the OU agent makes complementary observations on how much of the resource it received and how long it had to wait. If the XVO values computed as a result are low, then adaptivity may modify the parameters of the request, causing the OU to request from a different SU.

ECLAIR agents also represent supply units. Behavior for re-supplying supply units is similar to operational units, except that SUs will send an asset to a ship (circle labeled "AR") instead of sending a request to another unit. The assets include trucks (circle containing a box) and helicopters (hemisphere containing a bow-tie). For these simulations, we concentrated on adaptivity of OUs, although the capabilities to adapt SU behavior were available.

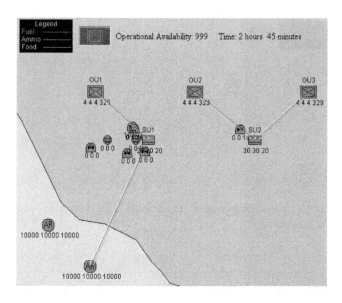

Fig. 4. The ECLAIR logistics demonstration before adaptation (beginning of simulation). OU2 and OU3 order resources from default supply unit (SU2).

Figure 4 depicts a scenario where the left-most SU, *SU1* has nine assets and the right-most SU, *SU2* has only one. The OUs, (*OU1, OU2,* and *OU3*) are initially assigned a default supply unit to order resources from. By default, OU1 requests resources from SU1 and OU2 and OU3 request resources from SU2. In Figure 4, the arrows from OU2 and OU3 show requests for resources being made to SU2. The demonstration uses the concept of Operational Availability (AO) as a metric in evaluating speed of command. A high AO score indicates that units are being supplied when needed. A low score indicates undesired delays.

5.2   Results

Figure 5 shows the typical results of the demonstration scenario. In our first scenario SU2 was "handicapped" in that it only had one asset, compared to SU1's nine assets. In order to add an element of instability in the environment, pop-up enemy units periodically attacked OU3, causing a sudden increase in the need for ammunition. In most runs of this scenario, AO initially decreased rapidly until the ECLAIR agents learned to choose different supply units based on the availability of resources. Within a short period, OU2 and OU3 learned to decrease the expectations of SU2's reliability because it had only one asset. Also, as wellbeing decreased, more exploration occurred, causing the OUs to send their requests to SU1. Eventually, OUs almost always requested from the SUs that gave the right types of resources in the shortest period of time. In our demonstration prototype, we show that the ECLAIR agent framework provides solutions to SRL challenge problems; agents improve the speed of command and adapt to the changes in a demand driven network. Figure 6 shows the average AO score of 30 runs for three scenarios; *Default*, *Explore*, and *Adapt*. These scenarios were all based

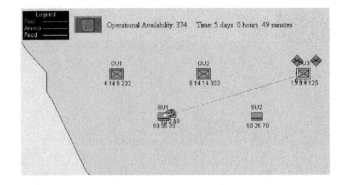

Fig. 5. The ECLAIR logistics demonstration after adaptation. OU3 learns to order resource from SU1 because it is more reliable.

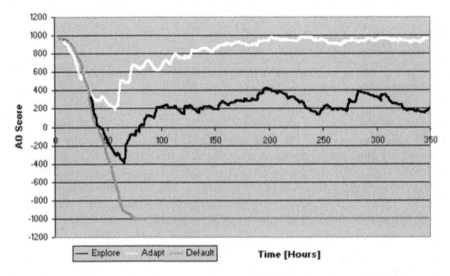

Fig. 6. Average AO scores for 30 runs, over a period of 350 simulated hours. The dark gray line shows the score of the default behavior. The black line shows the score using random exploration. The white line shows the score using adaptivity.

on the scenario described previously. The dark gray line, marked "Default," shows the results of agents only requesting supplies from their default supply units. The black line, marked "Explore," shows the results of agents selecting a random supply unit at an exploration rate based on wellbeing, but not using learning results to adapt. The white line, marked "Adapt," shows the results of agents using learning results to adapt.

In the *Default* scenario, agents only used their default behavior. In *Explore*, the agents may have randomly chosen the best supply unit to request to, but they were not making selections based on learned knowledge. The AO scores for the *Adapt* scenario were considerably higher than the other scenarios. *Default* quickly bottoms out at the lowest possible score. *Exploration* only reaches an AO score of around 400, while *Adapt* flattens out near 1000, the maximum score.

The graph in Figure 6 shows that using learning to adapt to the environment yields a clear improvement in speed of command. The need for fuel, ammunition, and food varied from hour to hour in all scenarios. At the end of the *Adapt* scenario, OU2 and OU3 were being supplied faster by asking a more responsive SU1 for supplies. The speed of command was improved from its initial setting when SU2 was supplying all of the needs to both OU2 and OU3.

Our final scenario shows agent adaptation to dynamic changes in the environment. We set up a contrived scenario in which resource availability for supply units changed drastically over time. In the scenario, OU3 sent requests to SU1 by default, however SU1 initially had no ammunition and took several days to order more. SU2 had a stock-pile of ammunition, but it could not send assets to get more when it ran out. In order to show that OU3 was adapting to the changes in the environment, it should first learn to request resources from SU2, but should later switch to SU1 after SU2 runs out of ammunition. Figure 7 represents a typical run of this scenario. The graph indicates when (x-axis) and to whom (y-axis) OU3 sent requests for ammunition. The vertical lines indicate events that changed the environment in the scenario. The events are:

1. Begin. SU1 has no ammunition, but SU2 has 75 units of ammunition
2. Enemy appears
3. SU1 receives 100 units of ammunition
4. SU2 runs out of ammunition and does not order more

OU3 did learn to adapt to the changes in the environment. At first it made four requests for ammunition from its default supplier, SU1, but then learned to make requests to SU2. After SU2 ran out of ammunition, OU3 explored and made a request to SU1 around day six. At around day nine OU3 learned to continue making requests to SU1, and did so almost exclusively. The exception was an exploration at around day 15 due to a non-zero exploration rate. However, when averaging over multiple runs, variations such as these do not change the overall effect. This scenario shows that adaptivity occurs quickly enough to respond to frequent changes in the environment. For example, OU3

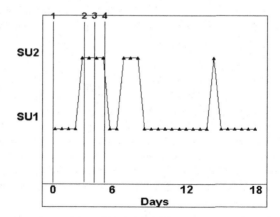

Fig. 7. Results from a scenario depicting several events that cause OU3 to adapt its behavior. OU3 learns to send request to SU1 or SU2, depending on their resource availability.

learned to request from a different SU after only four interactions with the environment. Our goal for future work is to use agent coordination and cooperative learning to improve the speed of command even more.

6   Current Work

We are currently working on a method to expand goal-based adaptivity into multi-agent coordination. Agents will use an associative memory technique to pull relevant objects from their memory that contains knowledge about agents and objects in the world. Associations can represent groupings of objects, or coordination structures that are used as the basis to generate plans for agents. Coordination structures are adapted to new situations using an extended constrained clustering technique. Preliminary results indicate that our technique works well considering a number of aspects including; rules to belong to a group, value of a group given its members, and cost to move objects from group to group. It also scales well to the number of agents expected in our scenarios. Developing an appropriate coordination structure is a collective process in which each agent involved in coordination will submit its possibly unique solution and all agents will decide on a final solution using an adapted voting technique. Accommodation works with multiple behavior types. In our previous work, we used accommodation to modify plan and reflex behavior. In our current work, we are using accomodation to modify coordinated behavior, which will manifest into modified agent plans.

7   Conclusion

We have developed a cognitive agent architecture that provides the framework for Sense and Respond Logistics. SRL requires coordination among agile, responsive units, and presents an optimization problem with a moving target. Our agent architecture will advance the current state of logistics applications because agents can follow the moving target by adapting to a changing environment. We presented initial results of a logistics implementation using the ECLAIR architecture that shows that adaptive agents have improved behavior over agents that do not adapt. We intend to continue extending the agent architecture and the military application to more fully address problems that arise in SRL and other net-centric operations.

Our agent architecture uses cognitive models based on Piaget's Cognitive-Stage Theory of Development [21] and Damasio's Somatic Marker Hypothesis [6]. Agents take a hybrid approach to action, using logic-based plan behavior in normal situations, and emotionally-inspired reflex behavior when they perceive internal distress. Adaptivity can manipulate plan and reflex behavior, improving agents' performance and increasing the speed of command. Our cognitive architecture is an excellent framework for SRL because plan behavior encourages agents representing warfighters to follow strategies built from experience in the battlefield, while reflex behavior helps the agents handle unexpected situations.

ECLAIR's unique contributions to agent research are the cognitively-inspired architecture that supports decision making using plan and reflexive behavior, and our net-centric approach to logistics. We are using adaptive agents to tackle the critical problems summarized by the Department of Defense [24] with an approach that is oriented towards SRL. ECLAIR bridges research in adaptive agents and cognitive architectures with the military domain that is just beginning to acknowledge the need for adaptive systems. We are also interested in making usable tools for real-life problems. At LM ATL, we have the proven capabilities to extend our research into the real world and supply practical applications for use by warfighters in the global theater.

References

1. ANDERSON, J. R., BOTHELL, D., BYRNE, M. D., DOUGLASS, S., LEBIERE, C., AND YULIN. An integrated theory of mind. *Psychological Review 111*, 4 (2004), 1036–1060.

2. BUCZAK, A. L., COOPER, D. G., AND HOFMANN, M. O. Evolutionary platform for agent learning. In *Proceedings of the Intelligent Engineering Systems Through Artificial Neural Networks* (New York, 2004), vol. 14, ASME Press, pp. 157–164.

3. BUCZAK, A. L., GREENE, K., COOPER, D. G., CZAJKOWSKI, M., AND HOFMANN, M. O. A cognitive agent architecture optimized for adaptivity. In submission to Artificial Neural Networks in Engineering (ANNIE '05).

4. COOPER, D. G. Context based shared understanding for situation awareness. In *Proceedings of the MSS National Symposium on Sensor and Data Fusion, 2004* (2004).

5. CZAJKOWSKI, M., BUCZAK, A. L., AND HOFMANN, M. O. Dynamic agent composition from semantic web services. In *Proceedings of the 2nd Workshop on Semantic Web and Databases (SWDB), 2004* (2004), pp. 1–14.

6. DAMASIO, A. R. *Descartes' Error: Emotion, Reason, and the Human Brain.* G.P. Putnam, New York, 1994.

7. DECKER, K. S., AND SYCARA, K. Intelligent adaptive information agents. In *Working Notes of the AAAI-96 Workshop on Intelligent Adaptive Agents* (Portland, OR, 1996), I. Imam, Ed.

8. DEFENSE AND THE NATIONAL INTEREST. *Fourth Generation Warfare.* http://www.d-n-i.net/second_level/fourth_generation_warfare.htm.

9. FRANKE, J., SATTERFIELD, B., AND JAMESON, S. Information sharing in teams of self-aware entities. In *Proceedings of the The Second International Workshop on Multi-Robot Systems NRL* (2003).

10. GERKEN, P., JAMESON, S., SIDHARTA, B., AND BARTON, J. Improving army aviation situational awareness with agent-based data discovery. In *Proceedings of the American Helicopter Society Conference* (2003).

11. HAYNES, T., WAINWRIGHT, R., AND SEN, S. Evolving cooperation strategies. In *Proceedings of the First International Conference on Multi–Agent Systems* (San Francisco, CA, 1995), V. Lesser, Ed., MIT Press.

12. HELSINGER, A., THOME, M., AND WRIGHT, T. Cougaar: a scalable, distributed multi-agent architecture. In *Systems, Man and Cybernetics* (2004), vol. 2, IEEE, pp. 1910–1917.

13. IOERGER, T. R., VOLZ, R. A., AND YEN, J. Modeling cooperative, reactive behaviors on the battlefield using intelligent agents. In *Proceedings of the The Ninth Conference on Computer Generated Forces (9th CGF)* (2000), pp. 13–23.

14. JONES, R. M., LAIRD, J. E., NIELSEN, P. E., COULTER, K. J., KENNY, P., AND KOSS, F. V. Automated intelligent pilots for combat flight simulation. *AI Magazine 20*, 1 (1999), 27–41.

15. KAELBLING, L. P., LITTMAN, M. L., AND MOORE, A. W. Reinforcement learning: A survey. *Journal of Artificial Intelligence Research 4* (1996), 237–285.

16. KOZA, J. R. *Genetic Programming: On the Programming of Computers by Natural Selection*. MIT Press, Cambridge, MA, 1992.

17. LEWIS, R. L. Coginitive theory, soar. Tech. rep., Ohio State University, Doepartment of Computer Science, 1999.

18. LITTMAN, M. L. Markov games as a framework for multi-agent reinforcement learning. In *Proceedings of the 11th International Conference on Machine Learning (ML-94)* (New Brunswick, NJ, 1994), Morgan Kaufmann, pp. 157–163.

19. LOCKHEED MARTIN ADVANCED TECHNOLOGY LABORATORIES. *Cooperative Agents for Specific Tasks (CAST)*. http://www.atl.lmco.com/overview/programs/IS/CAST.html.

20. LOCKHEED MARTIN ADVANCED TECHNOLOGY LABORATORIES. *Published Papers*. http://www.atl.lmco.com/overview/library.html.

21. MILLER, P. H. *Theories of Development Psychology*. W.H. Freeman and Co., 1983.

22. NASON, S., AND LAIRD, J. E. Soar-rl: Integrating reinforcement learning with soar. Tech. rep., University of Michigan, 2004.

23. NEWELL, A. *Unified Theories of Cognition*. Harvard University Press, Cambridge, MA, 1990.

24. OFFICE OF FORCE TRANSFORMATION, UNITED STATES DEPARTMENT OF DEFENSE. *Operational Sense and Respond Logistics: Coevolution of an Adaptive Enterprise Capability*, 2004. Concept document in progress.

25. SIMON, S. J. The art of military logistics. *Communications of the ACM 44*, 6 (2001), 62–66.

26. SUTTON, R. S. Reinforcement learning: Past, present and future. In *SEAL 1998* (1998), pp. 195–197.

27. SUTTON, R. S., AND BARTO, A. G. *Reinforcement Learning: An Introduction*. MIT Press, Cambridge, MA, 1998.

28. WOOD, R. J. Information engineering; the foundation of information warfare. Tech. rep., Air War College, Air University, 1995.

A Mobile Agent-Based Middleware for Opportunistic Resource Allocation and Communications

Marco Carvalho[1], Michal Pechoucek[2], and Niranjan Suri[1]

[1] Florida Institute for Human and Machine Cognition,
40 South Alcaniz St. Pensacola, FL, USA
{mcarvalho, nsuri}@ihmc.us
[2] Gerstner Laboratory, Czech Technical University,
166 27 Prague 6, Czech Republic
pechouc@labe.felk.cvut.cz

Abstract. Dependable communication capabilities are amongst the most important technical requirements for mission success in military combat operations. This paper introduces a mobile agent-based middleware that supports both point-to-point messaging and hierarchical data-streaming. Two infrastructure technologies (Mockets and FlexFeed) are introduced as service providers for messaging and publish-subscriber models for data streaming. Opportunistic resource allocation and monitoring are handled by distributed coordination algorithms, implemented here through two complementary technologies: Stand-In Agents and Acquaintance models.

1 Introduction

Communications in military battlefield operations are currently one of the most critical technical capabilities for mission success. From a network perspective, tactical military operations are often characterized by highly dynamic ad hoc wireless environments and include heterogeneous nodes under resource and security constraints. Furthermore, the communications infrastructure is expected to change its behavior and optimization criteria to adapt to changes in goals and priorities.

In recent years, a number of research efforts have focused their attention on this problem, looking for better routing or transport algorithms that would correct the deficiencies observed in the use of traditional wired network protocols.

Despite the invaluable progress these efforts have brought to the field, the reality is that in practice today networks are still deployed and configured in a customized fashion, to address specific needs or missions, with very specialized capabilities.

The problem is often associated with the notion that the communications infrastructure is expected to be completely isolated from the semantics of the data. Traditionally, this has been a very fundamental concept that provided portability and standardization of different network and communication protocols.

It seems clear, however, that mission-critical applications require not only the generality and flexibility inherent from context-free protocols, but also the efficiency provided by data-aware protocols, better able to create and maintain specialized data distribution trees in the network.

S.G. Thompson and R. Ghanea-Hercock (Eds.): DAMAS 2005, LNAI 3890, pp. 121–134, 2006.
© Springer-Verlag Berlin Heidelberg 2006

In this paper, we introduce a novel agent-based communications framework designed to help address the issue in these types of environments. The goal is to provide a middleware[1] that will overlay the physical network and transparently provide both services, with minimal changes in current software applications and systems.

In our framework, intelligent software agents are used to enable, on demand, data-aware capabilities in the network. The agents are mobile, so code and computation can be moved as necessary to opportunistically create capabilities and to react to changes in topology, resource availability, and policies.

The framework proposed in this paper leverages from a set of core technologies that have been designed and developed by our research teams for similar types of scenarios. Extensively tested in numerous proof-of-concept applications and demonstrations, these technologies have matured to a point where they complement each other to enable the framework.

2   Capabilities and Components

The communications middleware proposed in this work provides three core capabilities: support to point-to-point messaging; publish-subscribe oriented data streaming, and on-demand, opportunistic resource allocation. The idea is to combine the context-specific and context-free communication requirements supported by two APIs (Mockets and FlexFeed) into a common communications middleware, so they can leverage from a common resource management infrastructure.

The Mockets API provides a TCP-like interface to the applications. The API can be used to exchange general purpose message or streaming data. The FlexFeed API provides a publish-subscribe interface to applications. FlexFeed is responsible for handling data-aware data-streams, leveraging from the opportunistic allocation of resources provided by the coordination components. Both FlexFeed and Mockets are regulated through distributed (or centralized) algorithms, implemented as coordination components that identify, configure, and allocate resources in the network.

The coordination components constitute the "intelligent" part of the framework. They are responsible for sharing state between neighbor nodes and for negotiating the temporary allocation of resources necessary to support FlexFeed and Mockets.

Furthermore, the coordination components are also responsible for determining the appropriate course of action or recovery measures to be taken when changes in network topology or resource availability interfere with the communication tasks.

As a distributed component, the issues involved in resource coordination tasks are critical and complex. In the next section the basic technologies involved in the coordination components and the communication APIs will be discussed in greater detail.

3   Design and Implementation

The framework is implemented in Java. Each of the components integrated in the framework have their own access API which is used by external applications and between components to exchange services and state.

---

[1] The terms "Framework" and "Middleware" are used interchangeably in the context of this publication.

In order to support the capabilities required by the framework, it is important to have access and control of the underlying ad hoc routing protocol. Currently, an application-level implementation of a customized version of AODV [1] is integrated with the framework.

The coordination components use routing information and costs from multiple paths (from the underlying routing component) to identify possible data distribution trees that will lead to approximate global optimization of joint or disparate streams.

Figure 1 shows a diagram of the main components of the framework. In the figure, the physical node block represents the actual hardware platform, including the radios and the data-link layer.

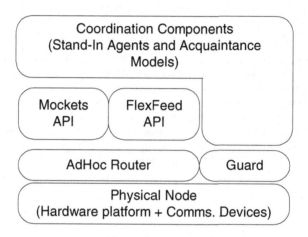

Fig. 1. Framework Components

The Guard is a software component with direct hardware access to provide local enforcement of policies and resource utilization. The middleware is integrated with a policy framework (KAoS) [2, 3] that provides the mechanisms for policy definition, verification, distribution, and enforcement, done at each node by the Guards.

The Guard components are responsible for maintaining and enforcing constraints and obligations in the local host. In the proposed framework, the Mockets and Flex-Feed components work as local enforcers on data-streaming and message related policies. When necessary, these components will query the local Guards for policy information so the coordination components can take the constraints into account when building a specific solution. Resource utilization by all other processes in the local host (like applications and agents) is directly enforced, at a lower level, by the Guards. Together, Mockets, FlexFeed and the Guard components ensure that all host level operations are within policy constraints, even if the policy repository is temporarily inaccessible to the node.

The coordination components are the entities responsible for negotiating and determining resource distribution both at the local and global levels. These components have direct access to the guard interface (for policy querying) and to underlying routing and transport protocols for parameter estimation.

During resource negotiation with peers, the coordination components also check policy constraints with the KAoS framework (through Guards interface). Both at the level of resource utilization and information release, constrains are enforced by the selective deployment of agents. To a certain extent coordination components are responsible for policy enforcement at the framework level in the same way that guards, FlexFee and Mockets are responsible for local policy enforcement.

3.1 FlexFeed

FlexFeed [4], in the context of this framework, provides the mechanisms to configure and task network resources in order to deploy the allocation schemes determined by the coordination components. FlexFeed was initially designed and tested as a middleware for data distribution in military operations (as part of a previous research effort sponsored by the Army Research Laboratory).

The framework relies on mobile software agents to transparently enable capabilities in network nodes for data processing and distribution between multiple (possibly disparate) applications.

The FlexFeed framework provides a Java interface for stream-oriented communications between applications. Sensors and clients use the FlexFeed API to provide and access information feeds. The transport mechanism, the message distribution, and filtering are handled at the framework level, hidden from data producers and consumers.

Consider the case illustrated in figure 2. In this example, the Unmanned Aerial Vehicle (UAV) is the source of the data, as it carries a high resolution video camera aimed at enemy positions.

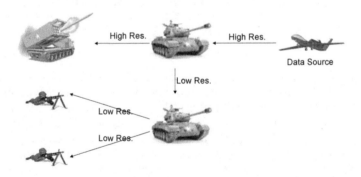

Fig. 2. Providing customized data-aware streams

In this example, a missile launcher requests a high resolution data-stream from the UAV to identify potential targets while at the same time, soldiers in the battlefield guarding the perimeter request visual data to monitor the movement of enemy troops.

The goal of the FlexFeed framework in this case is to identify the best data-distribution tree that would minimize overall transmission and data processing costs to support client requests.

Specialized agents, capable of transforming video data in this case, are injected in the framework at run-time (either by clients or by the source of the data). These agents can be positioned at any node in the network to establish the data distribution tree. FlexFeed interacts with the coordination components to identify the best resources available for the task.

With that information, FlexFeed then positions the agents accordingly and initiates the data-streams. From a minimum cost perspective, the best solution in the example shown in figure 2 is to send a high-resolution video stream to a nearby tank (with spare processing capabilities) that would then be responsible to clone and transform the stream, relaying the high resolution stream to the missile launcher and the low resolution equivalent to another tank near the soldiers for final distribution.

Once established, coordination components will continuously monitor the state of the network to react to changes in topology, resource availability, or policies. If necessary, the data-processing elements deployed in the first tank, for instance, can be moved to a sub-optimal position to re-allocate or release resources.

3.2 Mockets

Mobile Sockets (or Mockets) are an application-level transport layer specially designed to transparently provide resource redirection and cross-layer interaction in mobile ad hoc network environments. Mockets exposes a TCP-like interface implemented over UDP messaging and provides an extended API to support the exchange of state information and control messages between applications in the upper layers and underlying network protocols. Mockets were extensively used in a recent field exercise coordinated by ARL (Quantum Leap 2) to abstract complex underlying communication behaviors from applications that were originally designed to operate reliably over TCP.

The mockets communication framework provides a comprehensive communications API that addresses the limitation of TCP while at the same time offering new primitives for applications. To support existing TCP-style semantics, mockets provides a straightforward stream-oriented interface.

Applications written to use TCP can be easily modified to operate on top of the Mockets API. In addition, applications can take advantage of new capabilities such as keep-alive and connection statistics (bytes and packets sent as well as retransmission counts). The stream mockets implementation is designed to work on top of wireless and ad-hoc networks and does not exhibit the problems observed with TCP in such environments [8][9].

Mockets also provides a message-oriented interface. The message mockets support four different types of service: unreliable/unsequenced, reliable/unsequenced, unreliable/sequenced, and reliable/sequenced. The semantics of the unreliable/unsequenced service are similar to UDP and those of the reliable/sequenced service are similar to R-UDP. While there is no existing equivalent to unreliable/sequenced, this service is useful for situations such as video or audio streaming where packet dropout is preferred over out of sequence packets. Finally, the reliable/unsequenced service rounds out the set of capabilities.

When using the message-oriented paradigm, the mockets API provides additional features such as in-queue message replacement. This capability is particularly important for wireless networks and mobile ad-hoc networks where connectivity may be intermittent. It allows an application to replace a previous message with a new one, provided the previous message is still awaiting transmission in the mocket's outgoing queue. Messages may be tagged in order to classify them into different traffic categories. For example, if an application is sending periodic GPS position updates along with other traffic, the application can tag all the GPS position updates with a unique tag. When a new update is available, the application can simply ask mockets to replace any previous GPS update messages with the new one, which invalidates all the previous messages. This prevents large outgoing queues from accumulating when a node temporarily loses connectivity.

3.3 Coordination Components

The coordination components in the framework are the entities responsible for gathering state information to determine a cost-effective data distribution graph that will satisfy (within policies and resource availability constraints) the requests placed by each client.

In the types of environments considered in this work, global optimum allocation of resources is a very complex task, even for centralized algorithms with complete global information.

The complexity of the problem lies essentially in the fact that for each in-stream data processing configuration, network resources are affected, which leads to changes in the costs originally considered for the initial configuration as well as for all other active streams. The problem can be solved iteratively, with the risk of finding local optimal solutions and often 'hot-spots' in the data distribution paths.

There are, however, a number of heuristics and approximate cost functions that can be used to obtain a reasonable solution within the time scales required to make the framework practical. An example of a centralized approach to the problem is shown in [5], where a dijkstra-inspired algorithm is used to find an approximate solution.

Resource allocation in the framework is done through negotiation protocols, which requires p2p interactions between each host (and representative agent) involved in the transaction. This approach, however, is impractical for large scale systems due to communications overhead (for inter-agent negotiation) and transient partitions of the network caused by local link failures and changes in topology.

Furthermore, some of the candidate resources for data processing or communications relay might not be in communication range during the coordination process. There are many practical situations where this might occur, for instance if potential relays are mobile with a predictable path (like surveillance UAVs or ground vehicles), or in cases where nodes in strict passive mode (for instance, for security reasons) can be activated by framework if selected, or even cases where the framework is allowed to request nodes to physically move within communications range of other nodes to support temporary data-streams.

In cases like these, it is important for the negotiation procedures between coordination components to take into consideration temporary communications inaccessibility with potential candidates for the client requests.

The agent negotiation approach adopted in our framework is based on the notions of remote presence and remote awareness.

4   Remote Presence and Remote Awareness

In this section we discuss the techniques used in the framework to support the distributed negotiation process carried out by the coordination components.

The most critical cases include situations where coordination must account for environments that are temporarily unavailable (either by physical constraints, policies or choice), but the techniques can be easily extended to reduce communications overhead associated with the negotiation process.

The goal of the suggested techniques is to provide limited mutual awareness without the need for direct and continuous communication. The main applicability potentials are in the problems with a planning or a longer term coordination component. In such problem domains, the entities need to plan sharing resources and coordinate responsibilities, so that the joint goal can be effectively achieved.

Example 1. Let us have a computationally intensive task that needs to be decomposed and allocated to specific number of processors in a distributed, partially inaccessible environment. Without any knowledge of the services, current and planned load of the inaccessible processors, as much as the expected time when the connectivity can be established, the task would be delegated among the processors that are currently accessible. Awareness of the inaccessible processors allows planning the resource allocation on top of the inaccessible processors as well.

Example 2. Let us have a community of mine-sweeping underwater robots that are searching through the specific areas. The communication reach is restricted. Once a suspicious object is detected the robots need to position themselves into a communication feed so that the picture of the object can be transmitted successfully to the human operator. With the limited number of available robots, forming the communication feed is only possible if the agents maintain their approximate knowledge about each other location.

We distinguish among two types of techniques that can be used in the situations of communication inaccessibility:

- **remote awareness**, a set of techniques for representing the agents knowledge about the other inaccessible agents.
- **remote presence**, the concept of migrating the computational representative before the inaccessibility situation happens.

4.1   Acquaintance Models

The acquaintance models and computational models of the mutual awareness of the network elements (hosts, devices, routers, etc.) have been thoroughly studied and investigated in the area of agent technologies and agent-based computing. Each computational agent in the interaction environment is supposed to form (either collaboratively or individually) models of the other computational agents in terms of their location, load, plans and resource commitments, interaction accessibility, etc. This knowledge can be used for distributed coordination, planning for cooperation and resource commitments of the individual computational agents (of any kind).

The concept of acquaintance models have been exploited in modeling coordination in the semi-trusted environment of the OOTW domain within an AFRL funded project and for underwater mine-sweeping simulation project funded by ONR.

The acquaintance model does not need to be precise and up-to-date. Agents may use different methods and techniques for maintenance and exploitation of the acquaintance model. There has been various acquaintance models studied and developed in the multi-agent community, e.g. tri-base acquaintance model [6] and twin-base acquaintance model [7]. In principle, each acquaintance model is split into two parts: self-knowledge containing information about an agent itself and social-knowledge containing knowledge about other members of the multi-agent system. While the former part of the model is maintained by the social knowledge provider (an owner), the latter is maintained by the social knowledge requestor (a client). Social knowledge can be used for making operation of the multi-agent system more efficient. The acquaintance model is an important source of information that would have to be repeatedly communicated otherwise. Social knowledge and acquaintance models can also be used in the situations of agents' short term inaccessibility. However, the acquaintance models provides rather 'shallow' knowledge, that does not represent complicated dynamics of the agent's decision making, future course of intentions, resource allocation, or negotiation preferences. This type of information is needed for inter-agent coordination in situations with longer-term inaccessibility.

4.2 Stand-in Agents

An alternative option is to integrate the agent self-knowledge into a mobile computational entity that is constructed and maintained by the social knowledge provider. We will refer to this computational entity as a stand-in agent. The stand-in agent resides either on the same host where the social knowledge requestor operates or in the permanently accessible location. While using stand-in, the social knowledge requestor does not create an acquaintance model of its own. Instead of communicating with the provider or middle agent, it interacts with the stand-in agent. Therefore, the client agent is relieved from the relatively complex task of building and keeping up-to-date detailed acquaintance model and both provider and requestor may benefit from the full-fledged remote presence. Factoring the acquaintance model out of the each requestor agent's internal memory allows it to be shared between all locally accessible agents, further minimizing the traffic and computational resources necessary for model maintenance. The stand-in agents operate in three phases:

-   **stand-in swarming**, when stand-ins propagate through the system to reach the locations that may become inaccessible in the future. First, an existing stand-in agent or knowledge provider determines the set of currently accessible locations using a broadcast-like mechanism of the underlying communication infrastructure. Then, it may decide to create and deploy its clones on one or more of these accessible locations. After its creation, each deployed stand-in agent chooses the type of functionality it will provide in its location and repeats the evaluate/deploy process.
-   **information propagation**, sophisticated mechanisms for propagating the agent state updates (in terms of location, available resources, updated commitments) to its stand-in agents and synchronization within the community of the stand-ins. In

trusted communities synchronization is based solely on the freshness of the mode, while in non-trusted communities trust values also need to be considered.

- **conflict resolution**, when the stand-in agents synchronize their status (mainly in terms of the agreed commitments) with the formerly inaccessible agent. It often happens that the several stand-ins may have agreed on different commitments, which need to be resolved.

All three processes need to be tuned to the specific needs and properties of the given domain, such as the cost of communication, average accessibility among two agents, etc. The concept of stand-in agents is currently advantageous in the two very specific situations:

- in a very **dynamic environment**, with relatively low path accessibility (this can be in situations where a small number of unmanned vehicles are collaboratively inspecting large areas), or
- in a **non-trusted environment** with at least some communication inaccessibility (in these cases the agents do not want to provide sensitive knowledge for sharing while off-line).

Stand-in agents solve inaccessibility in two ways: the first is routing communication protocol based on swarming and micro-payments within agent community and the second is distribution of social knowledge. In this paper the authors talk about stand-ins without social knowledge functionality [10], because we want build only message passing system there. These stand-ins provide top-level communication API in mobile network.

An important attribute of the stand-ins is their passive role in the network. These agents are meant to be carried on a physical device and they aren't able to affect position of the device in mobile network anyway.

On the Figure 3, we present a sample stand-in agent network: nodes represent fixed locations, lines between nodes means that there exists a communication link between them and residing stand-in agent is represented by point near the node.

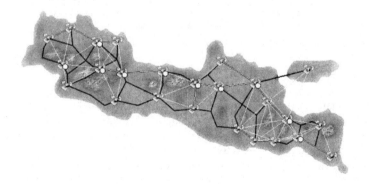

Fig. 3. An Illustrative Scenario

Unlike classical middle agent architectures [11] where the prime functionality is devoted towards matchmaking and negotiation, we would like to extend the concept of middle agent by its capability to autonomously migrate in the network, clone and destruct copies. Such extensions would allow us to better integrate the generic stand-in agent architecture with the coordination algorithms for the proposed framework. In Figure 4 we present an abstract architecture of the stand-in agent. The architecture presents the following components:

– **Swarming controller** consists of two modules: population manager ensures cloning; migration and destruction of stand-in agents in the system while the informationpropagator manages information flows through the agent, more specifically the messages or knowledge to transfer or actions to take. The module must balance between two extreme cases of knowledge handling: propagation to all visible targets or no propagation at all. Even if both modules are domain independent, they depend on the domain specific functions included in the knowledge base algorithms.

– **Knowledge base** is a domain specific knowledge structure of the stand-in agent, consists of three parts: activity knowledge, information evaluator and timeout checker. While the activity knowledge contains the domain specific knowledge and the meta-data provided by the propagator, the information evaluator and timeout checker are the algorithms working on this knowledge.

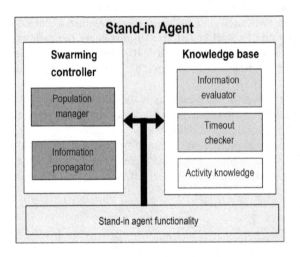

Fig. 4. Architecture of Stand-in agent

The information evaluator classifies and indexes the knowledge, so that the index values can be used by information propagator to manage its activity and further propagation. It also evaluates the knowledge usefulness. The timeout checker module implements forgetting of the activity knowledge.

– **Stand-in agent functionality** is the universal interface between modules and agent platform. It provides fundamental agent functions (clone, migrate and die), message interface and monitoring listeners, as well as original stand-in agent code. This code depends on the actual type of the stand-in agent. Via monitoring listeners it notifies modules about visibility of the other nodes, information about accessible other stand-in agents and also about presence of potential message receiver. Only this part of relay agent needs to be changed to work properly with another agent platform.

Combined, these capabilities allow the stand-in agent to provide the basic infrastructure for a distributed negotiation-based coordination component for the framework. In the following illustrative example, we illustrate the necessary steps involved for resource negation and allocation for a single data stream between a provider (source) and two consumers (sinks).

5 Illustrative Scenario

An illustrative application scenario is shown in figure 5, where a schematic view of a combat operation is presented. The figure illustrates a scenario with nine interconnected hosts. In the battlefield, each of these hosts might represent tanks, robotic vehicles, or soldiers. Each computational host (or environment) can execute a number of applications (or agents) represented in the figure as circles connected to the environment where they are executing.

Consider the case illustrated in figure 5 where clients (A) and (B) residing respectively in hosts H3 and H8 place a request for a specific data-stream from the same sensor application (S) executing in host H1.

Furthermore, consider the situation where the requests are different (but derivable from) each other. This would be the case, for instance, of client (A) requesting continuous GPS position information from sensor (S – presumed to be a UAV), while client (B) requests only low rate information for visualization purposes.

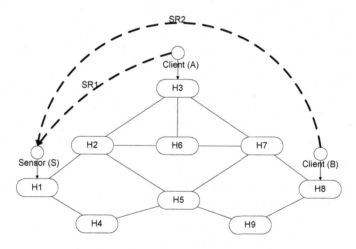

Fig. 5. An Illustrative Scenario

In this example, the order in which each request is place should not (in theory) change the final data distribution graph, as regardless of order, a final optimal solution will always be sought. However, in practice, the order does matter because changes in data distribution trees are based on changes in cost thresholds. That is, unless there are significant cost gains in moving from one solution to another, the system tends to preserve the current configuration.

Let us assume, for the purpose of this illustration, that both requests are placed simultaneously, represented in figure 5 by the dotted edges oriented from the "requester" to the "source" node. Conversely, the actual data streams in this illustration will be represented by solid arrows from the source node to the sinks (original requesters).

When receiving the requests, the sensor node (represented here as the agent – S) will start the policy verification and negotiation process to determine best allocation of resources.

First, the agent will query the local guard for policy constraints that might restrict communications or information release between the source and sink agents. The Guard will relay the query to the policy framework, and will then parse, cache, and return the results. Cached information will be used by the Guard to answer future policy queries in situations when the policy framework is temporarily inaccessible.

If there are policies constraining communications, for example between the sensor agent (S) and the client (A), these are automatically enforced in the form of changes in request parameters or automatic insertion of policy enforcement agents (or filters) in the data path. To simplify the example, let us consider the case where there are no policy constraints in place.

In this case, the sensor (S) will start negotiating resource allocation with other environments. Due to the incomplete connectivity inherent to these types of networks a protocol that would actually support agent negotiation between peers would be very expensive (in terms of messages exchanged) and possibly highly inefficient. Furthermore, during the negotiation process, there might be potential candidate nodes that are temporarily out of range, or in passive mode.

As discussed in section 4, the negotiation of resources in the framework can be done through two different mechanisms: Stand-In agents or Acquaintance Models. Different scales and types of scenarios might benefit from utilizing one approach or the other.

Consider for instance the case where Stand-In agents are used for resource negotiation. In this approach, a representative of each environment is either present at host H1, ready for negotiation, or are directly accessible (at low communication costs) by other representatives resident at H1. Information about data transmission and processing costs can be queried, on demand, by agent (S) to representatives of candidate nodes. Stand-In agents can also make resource commitments on behalf of their environments.

Armed with that information, agent (S) can identify resources in the network that can be tasked for data transmission or processing. Selected environments are then notified and configured for the task.

Figure 6 shows a schematic view of the data distribution stream established by agent (S) in coordination with its peers. It is important to note that in cases where (S) is a node highly constrained in computational resources, the negotiation process can be moved to a neighbor node (for instance H4).

Once established, the data-stream (or streams) will persist until canceled by the clients, or blocked by policies. In the case where changes in policy or topology might temporarily break sections of the stream the local agent in the affected node is responsible for corrective actions to quickly reestablish the data flow. For instance, if the communications edge between hosts H5 and H7 is dropped, agent R1 immediately starts a negotiation process to reestablish the link with R2.

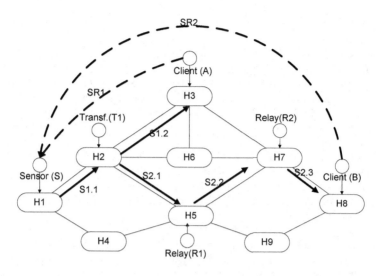

Fig. 6. A data distribution example

Periodically, agents re-evaluate local decisions with their peers, to find new local optima in cases where differences in cost are high enough to justify the changes. In this example, there is no global optimization between multiple sources.

6 Conclusions and Future Work

In this paper, a conceptual description of a mobile agent-based framework was presented for military battlefield environments. The framework provides three core capabilities: a) point-to-point messaging between applications; b) a publish-subscribe oriented model for data streaming, and c) on-demand, opportunistic resource allocation for communications and in-stream data processing.

Our approach relies on four core technologies that combined provide the features necessary to address the requirements demanded by the environment. Mockets and FlexFeed provide the application level access to the middleware, exposing the APIs for messaging and access to data-streams. Stand-In agents and Acquaintance models are presented as instances of remote presence and remote awareness capabilities (respectively), fundamental for a robust and truly distributed coordination model.

Although we currently don't have a fully integrated version of the framework, based on several examples of actual deployment and on a number of experiments conducted with each component independently (and some combined in ad hoc tests), we are confident of the capabilities that such middleware can provide to the types of scenario addressed here. Future work will involve the integration of coordination components with the rest of the framework to build a prototype for tests and demonstrations. We also plan an extensive set of tests and experiments to validate the concept and characterize the prototype.

References

1. Perkins, C. (2003). Ad hoc On-Demand Distance Vector (AODV) Routing. IETF – IETF Request for Comments (*RFC3561*).
2. Bradshaw, J.M. et al.: KAoS: Toward an Industrial-Strength Generic Agent Architecture. Software Agents, AAAI Press/MIT Press, Cambridge, Mass. 1997, pp. 375-418.
3. Bradshaw, J. M., et al. (1999). Agents for the masses: Is it possible to make development of sophisticated agents simple enough to be practical? IEEE Intelligent Systems(March-April), 53-63.
4. Carvalho, M. and Breedy, M. (2002) Supporting Flexible Data Feeds in Dynamic Sensor Grids Through Mobile Agents. Proceedings of the 6th International Conference on Mobile Agents (MA 2002). Barcelona, Spain. Berlin: Springer-Verlag
5. Carvalho, M. et al. (2005) The ULM Algorithm for Centralized Coordination in FlexFeed. To appear in the proceedings of the 9th World Multi-Conference on Systemics, Cybernetics and Informatics – Orlando (USA) - 2005
6. Pechoucek, M., Marık, V. and Stepankova, O. Towards reducing communication traffic in multi-agent systems. Journal of Applied Systems, 2(1):152-174, 2001. ISSN 1466-7738.
7. Cao, W.,. Bian, C.G., and Hartvigsen. G. Achieving e cient cooperation in a multi-agent system: The twin-base modeling. In P. Kandzia and M. Klusch, editors, Cooperative Information Agents, Number 1202 in LNAI, pages 210-221. Springer-Verlag, Heidelberg, 1997.
8. Cordeiro, C., Das, S. and Agrawal, D. COPAS: Dynamic Contention-Balancing to Enhance the Performance of TCP over Multi-hop Wireless Net-works", Proceedings of IC3N'02, Miami, FL, Oc-tober 2002
9. Gupta, A., Wormbecker, I, Williamson, C., Experimental Evaluation of TCP Performance in Multi-Hop Wireless Ad Hoc Networks. The IEEE Computer Society's 12th Annual International Symposium on Modelin, Analysis, and Simulation of Computer and Telecommunications Systems (MASCOTS'04). October 2004, The Netherlands.
10. K. Sycara, J. Lu, M. Klusch, and S. Widoff. Dynamicservice matchmaking among agents in open information environments. ACM SIGMOID
11. D. ˇSiˇslˊak, M. Rehˊak, M. Pˇechouˇcek, and P. Benda. Optimizing agents operation in partially inaccessible and disruptive environment. In Intelligent Agent Technology, 2005 IEEE/WIC/ACM International Conference, number PR2416 in IEEE, 200

Armed Services:
Challenges for Military Distributed Systems

David N. Allsopp

QinetiQ, St. Andrews Road, Malvern, WR14 3PS, UK
dnallsopp@qinetiq.com

Abstract. This paper discusses the relevance of agent-based and service-based approaches to the technical and organizational transformation sought by modern armed forces. It describes the rationale for using these approaches, potential benefits, and challenges — which are both organizational and technical. It then identifies gaps and areas for research including service discovery, support for a wide range of interaction patterns, and operation over low-bandwidth networks.

1 Introduction

A number of military initiatives are under way to change the way in which armed forces operate; these include the UK Network Enabled Capability (NEC), the US Network Centric Warfare (NCW) and the NATO Network Enabled Capability (NNEC). As the titles of these efforts suggest, organisational transformation is expected to go hand-in-hand with technological transformation in the areas of networks and distributed systems.

Even without these aspirations for new ways of working, the armed services, like many large organisations, possess diverse collections of separately developed IT systems. These are largely "stovepiped" and do not interoperate, leading to duplication of functionality and of information. There was little choice but to develop these isolated systems due to separate funding streams and the absence of a central architecture.

If technology is to be any use to the military, it must support rapidly evolving organisations and diverse operations, with constantly changing user needs and unforeseen interoperability requirements. This requirement is all the more compelling now that many operations are carried out within international coalitions.

"Although the US increasingly relies on coalitions to achieve its military objectives, the technological infrastructure necessary to support this strategy has been lacking. The gulf between the desired and the possible is especially glaring in the area of command, control, and intelligence." [1]

Agent-oriented and service-oriented approaches show potential for addressing some of these challenges. A full discussion of the differences and similarities between services and agents is outside the scope of this paper, but autonomy and goal-directed behaviour are often regarded as distinguishing features. This paper describes recent work investigating the strengths and weaknesses of such approaches within a military scenario, and summarises lessons learned and challenges identified.

S.G. Thompson and R. Ghanea-Hercock (Eds.): DAMAS 2005, LNAI 3890, pp. 135–140, 2006.
© Springer-Verlag Berlin Heidelberg 2006

2 Projects

The issues summarised in this paper are derived from work on software agents in the DARPA Coalition Agents Experiment and work on Web Services for the UK MOD. Both projects made use of the fictional Binni scenario (http://www.binni.org) [2].

CoAX (http://www.aiai.ed.ac.uk/project/coax/) was a Technology Integration Experiment within the DARPA Control of Agent-Based Systems Programme (CoABS), focussed on runtime interoperability of heterogeneous systems [3,4]. This work continues in the Fast Connectivity for Coalitions and Agents Project (FastC^{2}AP), which aims to extend agent-based technologies to accommodate secure web services [5].

The Componentisation for Reconfigurable Virtual Systems (CRVS) project is part of the UK MOD research programme. Work has included a demonstrator using Web Services and Semantic Web standards, showing the rapid discovery, visualisation and selection of services by a ground unit as it avoids enemy forces, calling upon information resources and supporting fire from across the battlespace.

3 What?

In discussing the potential benefits of technologies, definitions are a constant problem. The term "Service" is highly overloaded, resulting in confusion even within expert circles, and the precise definitions of both "Service" and Agent" can provoke prolonged debate. The hype surrounding the term "Service-Oriented Architecture" (SOA) has led some commentators to reject it as almost meaningless [6]. Given that universally-agreed definitions seem unlikely, we must at least define terms within a particular discussion and avoid overloading them in that context.

It may help to emphasise the underlying principles that various approaches have in common; for example, proponents of a variety of integration techniques can generally agree on some principles of "loose coupling" such as:

- Vendor and platform independence
- Separation of interface from implementation
- Late-binding (dynamic lookup, not hard-coded addresses)
- Asynchronous and stateless messages (where possible).

4 Why?

Why might the military be interested in agents and services? Reasons include:

- Agility (achieving dominance by seizing the initiative)
- Interoperability (between systems and between allies)
- Reuse (of functionality and of information)

It hardly needs to be repeated that no approach is a silver bullet for building systems that can deliver these qualities in difficult environments, but they are clearly a step in the right direction — monolithic, stovepiped, proprietary, static systems have been tried and found wanting; the obvious opposites are modular, open, dynamic systems.

5 Which?

Which agents and services should be provided? This cannot be answered without taking into account the investment in legacy systems on which the military currently rely. Existing functionality needs to be exposed within new frameworks in a logical and usable way, but this must be balanced against performance.

Many legacy systems cannot realistically be modified. Wrapping these systems as agents or services has been demonstrated, although this does not solve the problem of duplication of information and consequent inconsistencies.

Experience from industry indicates that it is rarely feasible to migrate to new approaches all at once; particularly for large organisations. An incremental "harvesting" of shared functionality is favoured, to create a growing toolbox of services or agents. An evolutionary approach is being taken by the US Network Centric Enterprise Services (NCES) acquisition programme, for example [7]. Such an implementation is not a once-and-for-all job (almost by definition: the whole point of these new approaches is to adapt to constant change, so there is never an end-state).

6 Where?

If our systems consist of many distributed agents and services, where should be they physically and logically be located? There are serious practical considerations:

- Physical security of the actual hardware
- Who pays for the hardware and its maintenance?
- How is redundancy provided to ensure resilience?

It should be borne in mind that "the military" is not a single homogeneous organisation, and that the networks are diverse and global. For example, the bandwidth of different military communications links varies by perhaps nine orders of magnitude.

7 How?

How should distributed components interact over military networks? Many open questions remain, since very few organisations have genuine significant SOA or agent deployments yet. Tools for creating such deployments are only beginning to emerge for conventional networks, let alone deployed military networks.

7.1 Discovery

A key issue is that of discovery of components across heterogeneous, global networks. Most research on discovery assumes a relatively homogeneous Internet or LAN environment, and frequently uses centralised matchmakers or brokers.

The need for expressive metadata for describing components must be balanced against the bandwidth required to disseminate these descriptions over highly constrained, heterogeneous and mobile military networks.

7.2 Messaging Patterns

Another vital aspect is the messaging patterns required, from simple "Inform" or "Query-Response" up to long-lived multi-party processes. Both current web service standards, and most agent systems, focus on 1:1 interactions between pairs of components, but many real-world activities involve communication between larger groups. This is particularly true for situational awareness in military operations, and will become more significant with military aspirations for dynamically formed "Agile Mission Groups" rather than pre-determined force structures. Interesting interaction patterns include flexible publish-subscribe, one-to-many notification and many-to-one fusion and aggregation of information.

It seems likely that any comprehensive solution for the military will need a hybrid approach, taking on board paradigms such as event-based middleware [8].

7.3 Composition Patterns

Other patterns identified in our work concern the definition and composition of parts; for example:

- Assembly of services to perform a process or workflow
- Virtual services (the Façade object-oriented pattern [9])
- Entities that present multiple interfaces
- Introduction (passing the identity of one agent to another)

7.4 Standards

In the world of Web Services, standardisation is somewhat fragmented, with two standards bodies (OASIS and W3C), an interoperability group (WS-I) and industrial players releasing specifications independently. The agent community fares better with a single body (FIPA) but has not gained the high degree of interest and uptake achieved by Web Services.

7.5 Security

There is often a lack of clarity when discussing security. It is important to distinguish:

- The accreditation of specific products for use in some context
- Vulnerabilities in specifications or language (such as SOAP or XML)
- Securing distributed systems (against who and what?)

Researchers developing agent algorithms for military applications will need to constantly consider ways in which their techniques can be defeated or subverted by an intelligent adversary.

Perhaps most interesting are the security issues inherent in open, interoperable, dynamic systems. In the past, accreditation involved defining a single profile of use for a closed system. This is untenable for systems where the components arrive, leave and change constantly, but formulating an alternative approach is an open problem.

The secure discovery of components is a new issue when systems are assembled on-the-fly. Physical or electronic attacks (such as denial of service) on discovery components could degrade or compromise the whole network.

8 When?

In the past, the timescales for acquiring new military systems have been very long; more open component-based systems offer the possibility of faster, incremental acquisition, in the style of iterative software development — but only if the military procurement organisations evolve alongside the technology.

At the other extreme, performance within and between computer systems is also an issue. Some applications require sophisticated real-time links; most general-purpose distributed technologies are unlikely to cope in these areas.

9 Who?

Such a radical change — from separately procured, separately managed systems, to highly distributed, intermingled applications assembled from a coherent set of modules — raises many organisational issues.

An application composed of services may effectively span multiple computers, across multiple military organisations. So, who is responsible for managing a particular service, especially if multiple copies of it exist in different places?

Separate programmes for each software system must give way to a coordinated, approach to procurement: new systems may require auditing and advice as they progress, to ensure re-use of existing components where possible, and to 'harvest' new shared components when overlaps emerge between projects.

10 Conclusions

Approaches based on loosely-coupled, communicating components — such as service or agents — offer significant benefits for military IT systems in terms of agility and flexibility, reuse of resources, and interoperability. However, organisational, information and process aspects are at least as important as the technology.

There are a number of gaps in the existing technology, particularly in the areas of robust, dynamic discovery of services across the battlespace, and also many-to-many interaction patterns such as publish-subscribe. These could be addressed by hybrid approaches using complementary areas of research in distributed systems. Some specific research gaps include:

- Tools for modeling and monitoring of wide scale systems
- Description and wide scale discovery of resources on heterogeneous networks
- Balancing interoperability and efficiency in very bandwidth-constrained networks.

Acknowledgements

QinetiQ work was carried out under the UK MOD research programme and also part funded by DARPA. We gratefully acknowledge all those who contributed to the CoAX project. The views contained herein are those of the author and should not be interpreted as necessarily representing official policies or endorsements, either expressed or implied, of the UK MOD, DARPA, or QinetiQ.

References

[1] Robert E. Marmelstein. "Force Templates: A Blueprint for Coalition Interaction within an Infosphere," IEEE Intelligent Systems, vol. 17, no. 3, pp. 36-41, May/June 2002.

[2] Rathmell, R.A. (1999) "A Coalition Force Scenario 'Binni - Gateway to the Golden Bowl of Africa'," in Proceedings of the International Workshop on Knowledge-Based Planning for Coalition Forces, (ed. Tate, A.) pp. 115-125, Edinburgh, Scotland, 10th-11th May 1999.

[3] Allsopp, D. N., Beautement, P., Bradshaw, J.M., Durfee, E.H., Kirton, M., Knoblock, C.A., Suri, N., Tate, A. and Thompson, C.W., "Coalition Agents Experiment: Multi-agent Cooperation in International Coalitions", IEEE Intelligent Systems, May/June 2002, pp 26-35

[4] Allsopp, D., Beautement, P., Kirton, M., Tate, A., Bradshaw, J.M., Suri, N. and Burstein, M. (2003) "The Coalition Agents Experiment: Network-Enabled Coalition Operations," Special Issue on Network-enabled Capabilities, Journal of Defence Science, Vol. 8, No. 3, pp. 130-141, September 2003.

[5] DARPA FastC^{2}AP: http://www.darpa.mil/ipto/programs/fastc2ap/

[6] Martin Fowler, Service Oriented Ambiguity
http://martinfowler.com/bliki/ServiceOrientedAmbiguity.html

[7] Defense Information Systems Agency, Net-Centric Enterprise Services
http://www.disa.mil/main/nces.html

[8] Peter R. Pietzuch and Jean M. Bacon. Hermes: A Distributed Event-Based Middleware Architecture. In Proc. of the 1st Int. Workshop on Distributed Event-Based Systems (DEBS'02), pages 611-618, Vienna, Austria, July 2002. See also http://www.cl.cam.ac.uk/Research/SRG/opera/publications/

[9] Design Patterns, Eric Gamma, Richard Helm, Ralph Johnson, and John Vlissides, Addison-Wesley Publishing Co., 1995; ISBN: 0201633612

Author Index

Lecture Notes in Artificial Intelligence (LNAI)

Vol. 3658: V. Matoušek, P. Mautner, T. Pavelka (Eds.), Text, Speech and Dialogue. XV, 460 pages. 2005.

Vol. 3651: R. Dale, K.-F. Wong, J. Su, O.Y. Kwong (Eds.), Natural Language Processing – IJCNLP 2005. XXI, 1031 pages. 2005.

Vol. 3642: D. Ślęzak, J. Yao, J.F. Peters, W. Ziarko, X. Hu (Eds.), Rough Sets, Fuzzy Sets, Data Mining, and Granular Computing, Part II. XXIII, 738 pages. 2005.

Vol. 3641: D. Ślęzak, G. Wang, M. Szczuka, I. Düntsch, Y. Yao (Eds.), Rough Sets, Fuzzy Sets, Data Mining, and Granular Computing, Part I. XXIV, 742 pages. 2005.

Vol. 3635: J.R. Winkler, M. Niranjan, N.D. Lawrence (Eds.), Deterministic and Statistical Methods in Machine Learning. VIII, 341 pages. 2005.

Vol. 3632: R. Nieuwenhuis (Ed.), Automated Deduction – CADE-20. XIII, 459 pages. 2005.

Vol. 3630: M.S. Capcarrère, A.A. Freitas, P.J. Bentley, C.G. Johnson, J. Timmis (Eds.), Advances in Artificial Life. XIX, 949 pages. 2005.

Vol. 3626: B. Ganter, G. Stumme, R. Wille (Eds.), Formal Concept Analysis. X, 349 pages. 2005.

Vol. 3625: S. Kramer, B. Pfahringer (Eds.), Inductive Logic Programming. XIII, 427 pages. 2005.

Vol. 3620: H. Muñoz-Ávila, F. Ricci (Eds.), Case-Based Reasoning Research and Development. XV, 654 pages. 2005.

Vol. 3614: L. Wang, Y. Jin (Eds.), Fuzzy Systems and Knowledge Discovery, Part II. XLI, 1314 pages. 2005.

Vol. 3613: L. Wang, Y. Jin (Eds.), Fuzzy Systems and Knowledge Discovery, Part I. XLI, 1334 pages. 2005.

Vol. 3607: J.-D. Zucker, L. Saitta (Eds.), Abstraction, Reformulation and Approximation. XII, 376 pages. 2005.

Vol. 3601: G. Moro, S. Bergamaschi, K. Aberer (Eds.), Agents and Peer-to-Peer Computing. XII, 245 pages. 2005.

Vol. 3600: F. Wiedijk (Ed.), The Seventeen Provers of the World. XVI, 159 pages. 2006.

Vol. 3596: F. Dau, M.-L. Mugnier, G. Stumme (Eds.), Conceptual Structures: Common Semantics for Sharing Knowledge. XI, 467 pages. 2005.

Vol. 3593: V. Mařík, R. W. Brennan, M. Pěchouček (Eds.), Holonic and Multi-Agent Systems for Manufacturing. XI, 269 pages. 2005.

Vol. 3587: P. Perner, A. Imiya (Eds.), Machine Learning and Data Mining in Pattern Recognition. XVII, 695 pages. 2005.

Vol. 3584: X. Li, S. Wang, Z.Y. Dong (Eds.), Advanced Data Mining and Applications. XIX, 835 pages. 2005.

Vol. 3581: S. Miksch, J. Hunter, E.T. Keravnou (Eds.), Artificial Intelligence in Medicine. XVII, 547 pages. 2005.

Vol. 3577: R. Falcone, S. Barber, J. Sabater-Mir, M.P. Singh (Eds.), Trusting Agents for Trusting Electronic Societies. VIII, 235 pages. 2005.

Vol. 3575: S. Wermter, G. Palm, M. Elshaw (Eds.), Biomimetic Neural Learning for Intelligent Robots. IX, 383 pages. 2005.

Vol. 3571: L. Godo (Ed.), Symbolic and Quantitative Approaches to Reasoning with Uncertainty. XVI, 1028 pages. 2005.

Vol. 3559: P. Auer, R. Meir (Eds.), Learning Theory. XI, 692 pages. 2005.

Vol. 3558: V. Torra, Y. Narukawa, S. Miyamoto (Eds.), Modeling Decisions for Artificial Intelligence. XII, 470 pages. 2005.

Vol. 3554: A.K. Dey, B. Kokinov, D.B. Leake, R. Turner (Eds.), Modeling and Using Context. XIV, 572 pages. 2005.

Vol. 3550: T. Eymann, F. Klügl, W. Lamersdorf, M. Klusch, M.N. Huhns (Eds.), Multiagent System Technologies. XI, 246 pages. 2005.

Vol. 3539: K. Morik, J.-F. Boulicaut, A. Siebes (Eds.), Local Pattern Detection. XI, 233 pages. 2005.

Vol. 3538: L. Ardissono, P. Brna, A. Mitrović (Eds.), User Modeling 2005. XVI, 533 pages. 2005.

Vol. 3533: M. Ali, F. Esposito (Eds.), Innovations in Applied Artificial Intelligence. XX, 858 pages. 2005.

Vol. 3528: P.S. Szczepaniak, J. Kacprzyk, A. Niewiadomski (Eds.), Advances in Web Intelligence. XVII, 513 pages. 2005.

Vol. 3518: T.-B. Ho, D. Cheung, H. Liu (Eds.), Advances in Knowledge Discovery and Data Mining. XXI, 864 pages. 2005.

Vol. 3508: P. Bresciani, P. Giorgini, B. Henderson-Sellers, G. Low, M. Winikoff (Eds.), Agent-Oriented Information Systems II. X, 227 pages. 2005.

Vol. 3505: V. Gorodetsky, J. Liu, V.A. Skormin (Eds.), Autonomous Intelligent Systems: Agents and Data Mining. XIII, 303 pages. 2005.

Vol. 3501: B. Kégl, G. Lapalme (Eds.), Advances in Artificial Intelligence. XV, 458 pages. 2005.

Vol. 3492: P. Blache, E.P. Stabler, J.V. Busquets, R. Moot (Eds.), Logical Aspects of Computational Linguistics. X, 363 pages. 2005.

Vol. 3490: L. Bolc, Z. Michalewicz, T. Nishida (Eds.), Intelligent Media Technology for Communicative Intelligence. X, 259 pages. 2005.

Vol. 3488: M.-S. Hacid, N.V. Murray, Z.W. Raś, S. Tsumoto (Eds.), Foundations of Intelligent Systems. XIII, 700 pages. 2005.

Vol. 3487: J.A. Leite, P. Torroni (Eds.), Computational Logic in Multi-Agent Systems. XII, 281 pages. 2005.

Vol. 3476: J.A. Leite, A. Omicini, P. Torroni, P. Yolum (Eds.), Declarative Agent Languages and Technologies II. XII, 289 pages. 2005.

Vol. 3464: S.A. Brueckner, G.D.M. Serugendo, A. Karageorgos, R. Nagpal (Eds.), Engineering Self-Organising Systems. XIII, 299 pages. 2005.

Vol. 3452: F. Baader, A. Voronkov (Eds.), Logic for Programming, Artificial Intelligence, and Reasoning. XI, 562 pages. 2005.

Vol. 3451: M.-P. Gleizes, A. Omicini, F. Zambonelli (Eds.), Engineering Societies in the Agents World V. XIII, 349 pages. 2005.

Vol. 3446: T. Ishida, L. Gasser, H. Nakashima (Eds.), Massively Multi-Agent Systems I. XI, 349 pages. 2005.